RECORDING THE PAST
A Photographer's Handbook

BY
ERIC HOULDER L.R.P.S.

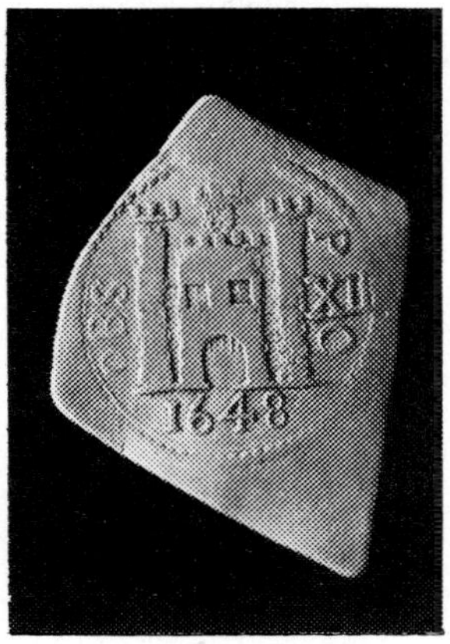

A LOCAL HISTORY SPECIAL
IN ASSOCIATION WITH
K. A. F. BREWIN BOOKS
STUDLEY 1988

Published jointly by K A F Brewin Books, Studley, Warwickshire B80 7LX and Susan and Robert Howard, Publishers, Local History, Devonshire Promenade, Nottingham NG7 2DS in March 1988.

ISBN No 0 947731 37 7

Typeset in Helios by D Graphic Services, Nottingham, England and made and printed in Great Britain by Sherwood Press, Nottingham, England.

BY THE SAME AUTHOR:

Digging for History in Pontefract
(Brewin Books 1988)

CONTENTS

List of Illustrations

All illustrations by Eric Houlder except:
No 3; W J Houlder
No 14; V J Houlder
Nos 19 & 20 and Nos 36 & 37 were taken by Eric Houlder on behalf of Wakefield Museums, Pontefract Museums (Maude Collection) and West Yorkshire Archaeological Service respectively.

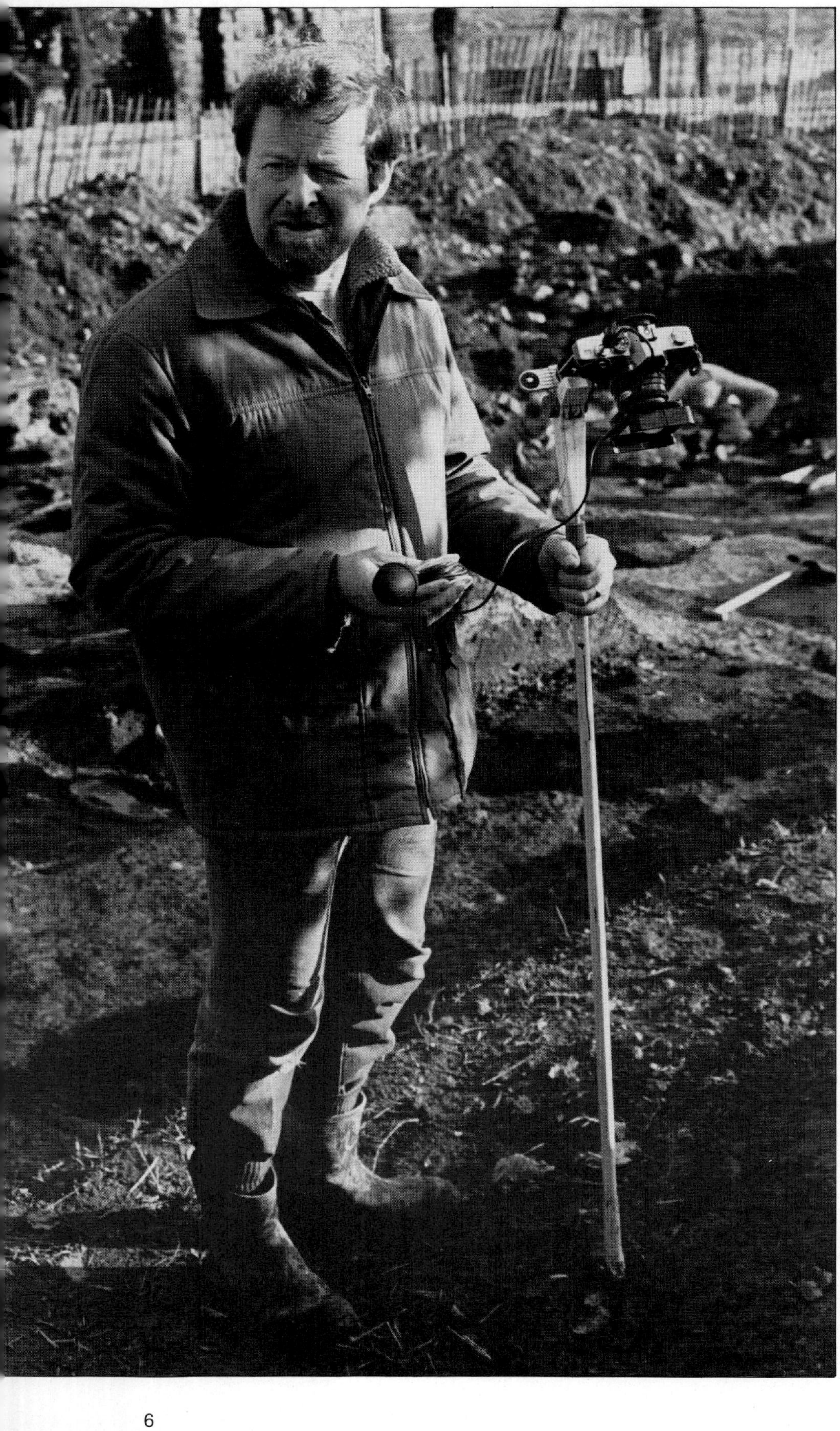

Eric Houlder

... is eminently qualified to be the author of *Recording the Past: A Photographer's Handbook;* he is head of History and Archaeology at The King's High School in Pontefract, West Yorkshire, and a Licentiate of the Royal Photographic Society (LRPS). He is also President of the Pontefract Camera Club, a past President of the Pontefract & District Archaeological Society and a past Chairman of the Castleford Historical Society.

Aged 46, Eric Houlder has combined his passions for archaeology, local history and photography in a number of ways; since the late fifties, he has taken part in numerous archaeological digs as a volunteer, supervisor and site director, including being area supervisor in charge of half of the Sutton Hoo Ship burial excavation, under Dr R L S Bruce-Mitford and Paul Ashbee, in 1969.

Eric's interest in archaeology and photography really took off when he became involved in aerial photography. In the past he has worked with Derrick Riley, one of the top half-dozen aerial archaeologists in Britain and author of numerous books and learned papers, and he has provided a number of well known authors with photographs for their books, including Plantagenet Somerset Fry (*Roman Britain*) and Keith Manchester (*The Archaeology of Disease*).

After coming second in the International Archaeological Photography Competition, which was organised by *Popular Archaeology*, Eric Houlder wrote a series of articles for the journal about photography.

More recently, Eric has contributed a series of articles on **Photography in Local History** to *Local History* and it is these articles, with some additional chapters and photographs which have provided the basis for *Recording the Past: A Photographer's Handbook.*

3. Eric Houlder.

Photography in local history: an introduction

Photography has been the Cinderella of local historical research for too long. Even today, some societies still regard a handful of trade-processed enprints as full photographic coverage of a research project which in all other respects is impressive. Yet with modern materials and equipment little real skill is needed to do an adequate job, whilst an extra effort can produce superlative results.

It was much harder and more expensive (comparatively) when I began taking an interest in local history nearly thirty years ago. As a fifth former with a morning milk round I had little time and money to devote to an interest which then (and now) I combined with an interest in archaeology. My first serious effort at recording was done almost by default! The society had undertaken to investigate and record a nineteenth century clay pipe factory in a derelict building. As the possessor of a new camera, and as no one else would do it, I took it upon myself to record the work. At great expense I purchased a flashgun, and bulbs. The film was processed and printed by a local professional who encouraged my interest. I became hooked! Shortly afterwards I bought a copy of M B Cookson's *Photography for Archaeologists*. Regrettably, at that time, there was no book available on photography in local history, so that most of the techniques I developed were adaptations of archaeological ones. The two disciplines have much in common, not the least important being the combination of enthusiasm and understanding necessary to achieve a first class photographic record.

In thirty years I have never lost the sense of adventure which must be inherent in this type of research record. Whether wriggling in eighteenth century mine-workings, leaning out of an aeroplane, grovelling in filthy cellars or standing over a rain-lashed Saxon burial group, I have never failed to get that feeling of awe which comes from knowing that my lens is recording something that has not been seen by living eyes for hundreds of years.

My advice to anyone just becoming involved in this fascinating field of photography is this. Never lose that sense of adventure; temper it with discipline, skill, and a little imagination. Help your long-dead subjects come across as living people, because, in the final analysis, that is what it is all about.

Eric Houlder
January 1988

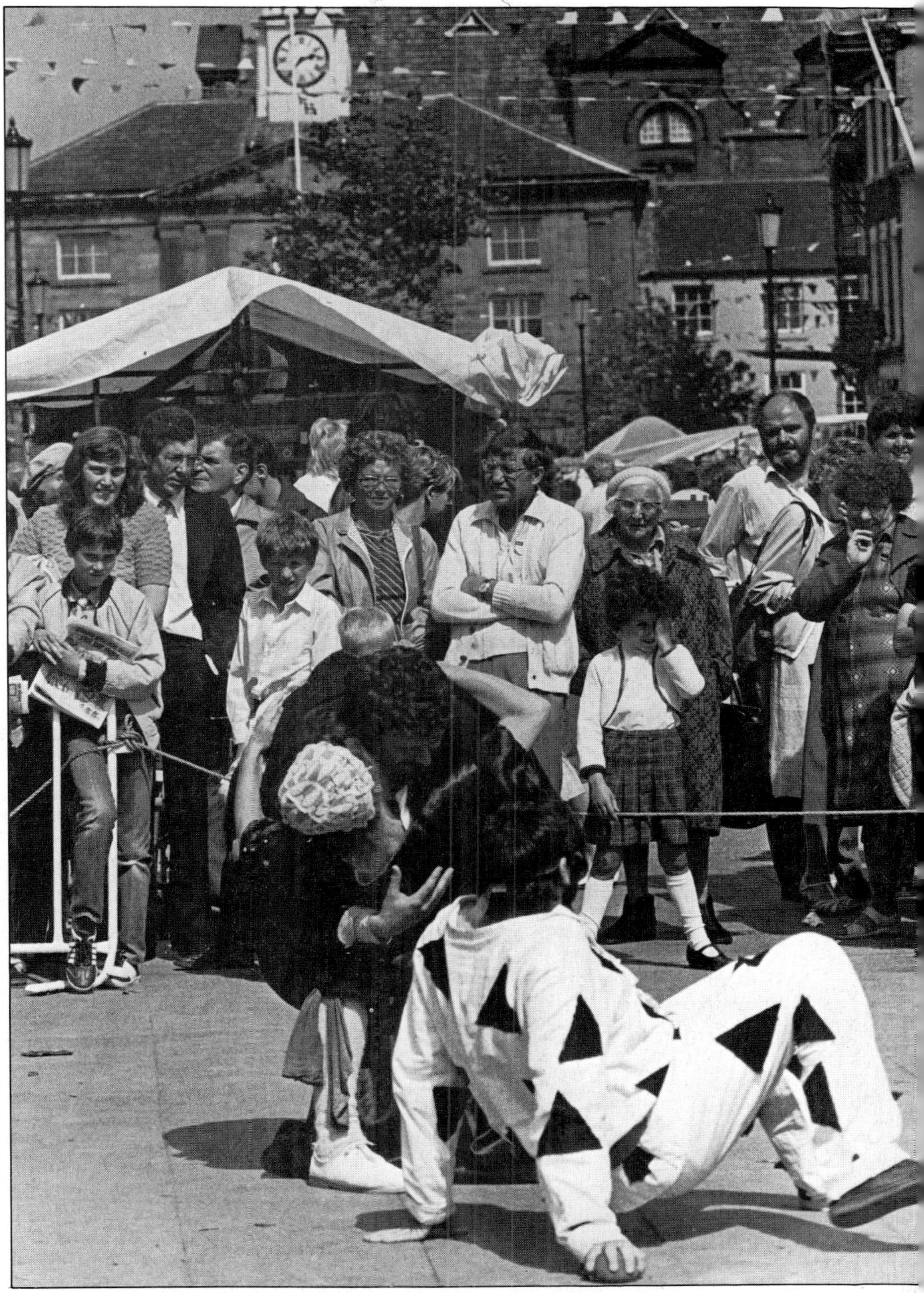

4. Street-players on Market Day. Notice how the photographer has focused on the audience, not the performers.

CHAPTER ONE

Scope and Equipment

Visit a photographic exhibition and you will find that the photographs are categorised. The usual categories are: pictorial (usually landscape); portraits; record and miscellaneous. As far as we local historians are concerned all our work falls into the record category, even if incidentally it includes elements of the others. However, do not despise the pictorial approach as it is important to make your pictures as attractive as possible because a pleasing composition will be of greater interest, and therefore of enhanced value, to future generations.

So what, in essence is photography? At its simplest it is a mechanical recording medium which, unlike all the other graphic media, does not depend on manual dexterity for the accuracy of its final result. It is superior to the graphic media because the camera is purely objective and records impartially everything before it. It can produce a variety of images which in themselves are capable of modification by filters, by chemical means, or mechanically, and which can be presented as reflection prints, diapositives (transparencies) or projected images.

With capabilities like this, photography should be the major tool of local history. In a few societies and groups it is, but in the majority it is still seen as either too complex to bother with, or worse, as a glorified seaside snapshot medium only.

Its scope in local history is enormous. A mere list of uses would be boring, but must be attempted if only to shake the complacency of those researchers who feel that they do not need to use it! Remember when reading through these subjects that each main heading will be in itself the topic of a future chapter:

The Historic Landscape
Recording Buildings
Recording People
Copying Documents and Pictures
Picturing Close-ups
Illustrating Books, Articles and Lectures
Aerial Photography
Basic Archaeological Photography
Industrial Archaeological Photography
The Simple Visual Notebook

With all these possibilities it would appear that the skilled local history photographer would need a variety of specialist cameras and other equipment. In fact all the subjects listed, with the possible exception of the last one, can be covered with one type of camera, the *35mm single lens reflex* or *SLR*. This type of camera will accept lenses of different focal lengths as well as apparatus for extreme close-ups. Flash equipment of various kinds can be attached, some of it giving faultless *automatic exposure*. Because viewfinding (the act of 'aiming') is always through the taking lens, and because in most modern types *exposure* is taken care of automatically, even the tyro can obtain usable results immediately.

In view of these considerations, what would the ideal local history outfit consist of? The first item should be a 35mm SLR, preferably from one of the big five Japanese manufacturers - Canon, Minolta, Nikon, Pentax or Olympus. Alternatively, choose from one of the two German companies still producing quality SLRs - Leitz and Contax. Rather than purchase the standard lens automatically with the camera, as most people still do, it is possible to buy a good quality *zoom* lens which will replace this and also provides a wide variety of other focal lengths too. A 28mm to 80mm zoom is an ideal lens for the local historian. This one lens would cover the recording of interiors, exteriors, documents, general scenes, moderate close-ups and even aerial photography. Though photographers of the old school look down their noses at zooms (and the present writer has done his share of this!) the zoom lens has now come of age. Good modern ones are the equal of *prime* (non-zoom) lenses for all intents and purposes, saving both money and weight. The 28 to 80 mentioned above would give the following conventional focal lengths: 28, 35, 45, 50, 70 and 80, as well as all the in-between settings, and moderate close-up capability too.

Beware of older zooms though. When they first came on the market in the sixties most were of poor quality compared with modern examples. Older prime lenses, in contrast, can be real bargains second hand. I still regularly use an ancient lens well over twenty years old which was designed for one of the original Minolta SLRs. These and similar optics are amazingly cheap in camera stores and are usually guaranteed too.

Many local history situations require the use of some form of extra lighting. The most conventional auxiliary lighting is, of course, *flash*. There are currently four types of flash equipment available, and most of them can find a use in our particular field. Oldest and now hardly used is the type of flashgun which used single bulbs filled with an inflammable mixture. These are expensive, difficult to buy in the useful sizes, but extremely powerful. Exposure must be estimated with the help of a table supplied with the bulbs. Unless you have some experience in photography with flashbulbs I do not recommend their use. Next in order of difficulty of use is the purely manual electronic flash (strobe in the USA). These guns are usually the cheapest, and hence the least powerful, in a manufacturer's range. Again, exposure must be estimated, but the user is generally assisted by a scale or calculator on the back of the gun. More useful if the auto/manual gun, which gives the user the option of an automatic exposure facility. When used within

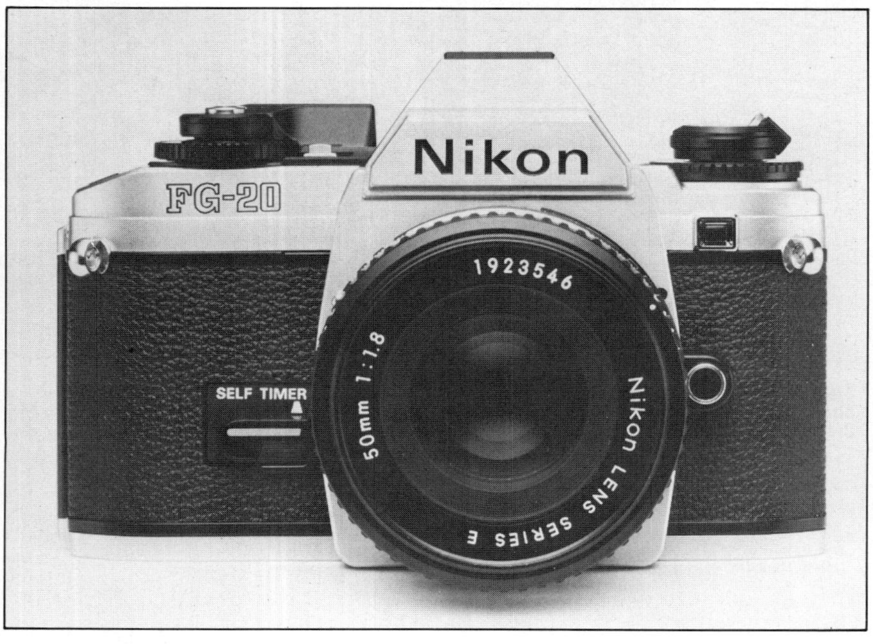

5. Single Lens Reflex (SLR) Camera.

their capabilities (which in effect means that the user must not try to take pictures of subjects beyond the flashgun's range) these can be the most useful. Lastly, there is the *dedicated* electronic flashgun. This type is the most sophisticated and is linked into the camera's electronics. When a photograph is taken, a sensor in the camera measures the light actually reaching the film and quenches the flash at the exact moment for a perfect exposure.

Whichever type of flashgun the local history photographer opts for, there are still some choices to be made. The most important of these is the power of the gun. There are two ways of measuring the output of an electronic flash. The older way is in Joules but this system is nowadays only used to describe the very large and powerful professional units. More common is the system of distinguishing by *guide number*. All manufacturers today quote a guide number for 100 *ISO* film. Alternatively, they may quote guide numbers for several speeds of film, but you can be sure that if no ISO speed is mentioned then 100 ISO is implied. The minimum power required for local history work is provided by a unit with a guide number of 30 metres or 100 feet.

The type of fixing point is also important. Most smaller units and all dedicated units are fixed to the camera's *accessory shoe* directly. The larger units are usually fixed to a substantial bracket which is then screwed into the tripod socket in the base of the camera. This latter type is much stronger and inspires more confidence when working in precarious positions. The advantages of the dedicated unit can still be used on this type of bracket by using a special dedication cord to link the unit and the camera's accessory shoe.

Some form of close-up accessory will also be found useful. The ordinary *macro* facility of a zoom lens should be quite adequate, but for anyone who feels that he/she may need to take extremely small subjects, a set of *extension tubes* will come in useful. Their use will be discussed in the chapter on close-ups.

Thus equipped, the enthusiast might think that he/she is the master of all he surveys, so a word of warning is appropriate at this point. Most photographs are not permanent; they fade! Worst in this respect are colour prints produced from negatives. Anyone wishing to achieve permanence in colour pictures is best advised to shoot on reversal film (for slides) and then print the resulting images onto *Cibachrome*, an Ilford process which utilises dyes of excellent keeping properties. Even better is to take photographs on conventional monochrome film, develop normally, and wash the negatives in running water for at least forty five minutes. With careful storage these should be usable well into the twenty-second century. To achieve permanence in black and white prints it is essential either to print them yourself to or pay a specialist. They must be on a high quality fibre-based paper, be washed to remove all traces of processing chemicals and then *toned* (either sepia or gold) and again washed thoroughly. Such services are not available commercially (except at a price), so the conscientious photographer must really be prepared to do everything.

Though most of us accept that our pictures will be of greater value in the future, we may also wish to use them today. The most obvious use is to illustrate books, articles, and lectures. For books and articles 10in x 8in, or A4 size, monochrome glossy borderless prints are required. Only rarely can smaller prints be submitted and, even then, certainly never smaller than 7in x 5in. If the original is a colour slide and monochrome reproduction is required, a 10in x 8in glossy Cibachrome is by far the best way to achieve quality.

Should you be lucky enough to have a picture published in colour, the printers will require a transparency, preferably on Kodachrome or Fujichrome 50. If you do not use either of these films do not despair. Excellent colour blocks can be made from the majority of modern high definition colour films, especially the slow ones, but most block makers are set up for the two films mentioned above.

For lectures and talks good colour slides are essential. The best quality pictures need a slow film (up to 100 ISO). Only when conditions deteriorate is it worth going on to a faster material. Try to stick to one make of film, if at all possible, as even today colour films from different makers have minor individual characteristics. These are not noticed when the slides are screened until two pictures of the same subject taken at the same time, but on different emulsions, are screened one after the other. All the major manufacturers make a range of films in different speeds, so the photographer is advised to try the different makes until he/she finds one that suits his/her tastes and then stick to it. For many years I used Agfa colour films, but about five years ago I changed to Fuji, as it had the type of colour rendering that I liked, together with improved sharpness. Since then

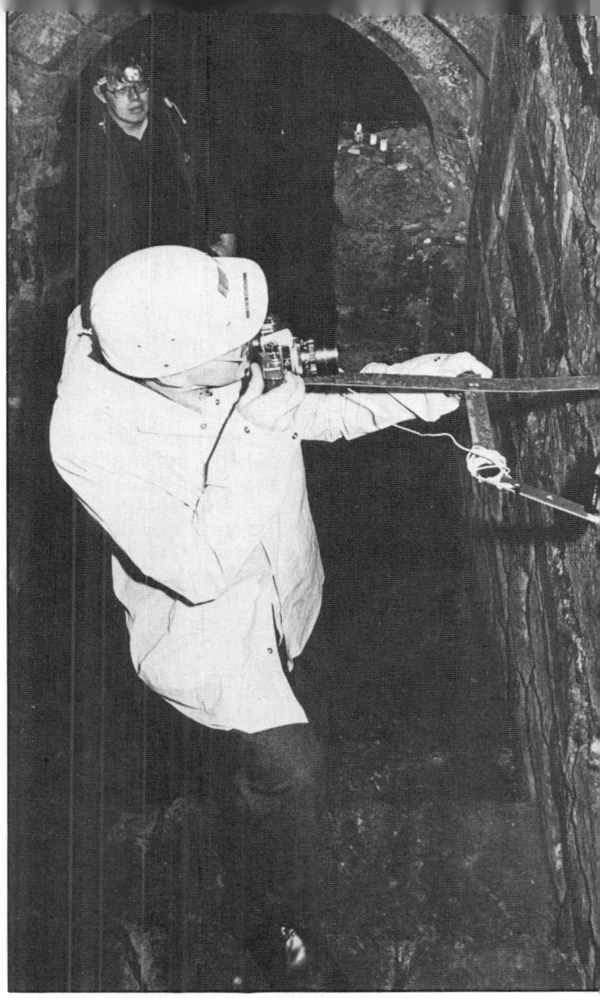

6. Recording graffiti in the dungeon, Pontefract Castle.

Agfa have modernised their films so it is quite likely that I shall change back! However, all the major brands are excellent and all can be relied upon to produce excellent results when used intelligently.

One of the problems of being the society photographer is the isolation. You can discuss local history with your friends in the group all day and all night but it is most unlikely that many of them will show much interest in the technical aspects of your photography. One way to avoid the problems that come with isolation is to join the local photographic society; this is the surest method I know of to improve the standard of your work. At a higher level there is the Archaeology and Heritage Group of the Royal Photographic Society, a miscellaneous collection of photographers with much the same interests as yourself. The Group publishes its own magazine and arranges conferences, workshops and lectures. At the time of writing its activities are confined to the south east. Membership is restricted to members of the Royal Photographic Society, but this is open to anyone. Members can, if they wish, submit work in order to gain the distinctions of **Licentiate**, **Associate** or **Fellow** of the RPS. These are internationally recognised as demanding high standards and entitle the holder to add the relevant letters to his/her name.

CHAPTER TWO

The Historic Landscape

The landscape has been a favourite subject with painters, and later photographers, since the Renaissance. Here in Britain we have a particularly rich tradition, so much so that reproduction Turners and Constables can be purchased even on market stalls! The advent of photography in the 1840s added a new dimension, and new landscape exponents, such as P H Emmerson in Norfolk, and Frank Sutcliffe in Whitby, made invaluable records. Alongside these giants of brush and lens many thousand lesser practitioners daubed and dabbled, so that there can be few districts with no old paintings, drawings, postcards or photographs.

In addition there are many aerial photographs in existence from the last sixty years. As well as showing the extant landscape these can give clues to past landscapes, the features of which may still be readable just below the present surface, like a palimpsest document.

This chapter suggests uses for old landscape studies in your research at different levels; shows you how to interpret clues to past landscapes in your photographs, and explains how to record existing ones.

Old pictures can come from several sources. The local history collection in your town or regional museum is a good place to start, but a visit to the lounge of an old people's home will usually produce large numbers too. Take a few old postcards with you to show around, and before long you will be inundated with all sorts of material. These items should be carefully copied and promptly returned. Copying is a straightforward photographic technique which is dealt with in chapter five.

Once you have assembled a collection of old topographical pictures comes the problem of what to do with them! Many groups like to publish them as booklets, and undoubtedly the best format is to print them as groups of series from old to new. Nothing emphasises the fascinating concept of change through time as much as a series of identical views taken, say, twenty years apart. The modern photographer's role in this is usually to re-photograph a view originally taken perhaps over a century ago.

Although this may appear to be a straightforward procedure, it is often not as simple as it sounds. Firstly the spot where the artist/photographer of the past stood must be identified. From here, with a copy of his picture, the precise field of view must be determined; very rarely will this match the exact field of view of a standard lens, hence the value of zooms. If no zoom is available then a wider lens must be used and the picture *cropped* at the enlarging stage. (Cropping is the removal of extraneous space from around the edges of a picture either by cutting or, in this case, by adjusting the enlarger easel to obtain the same effect. For those without darkroom facilities this service is available from any good photofinishers. Yellow Pages lists them, but do not expect to pay amateur rates for a professional service though.) For maximum sharpness you must emulate your

7. Windblown thin snow revealing ridge and furrow on the scarp edge across the centre of the picture. Darrington (Yorks).

Minolta SR1v. 100mm lens. Ilford HP5.

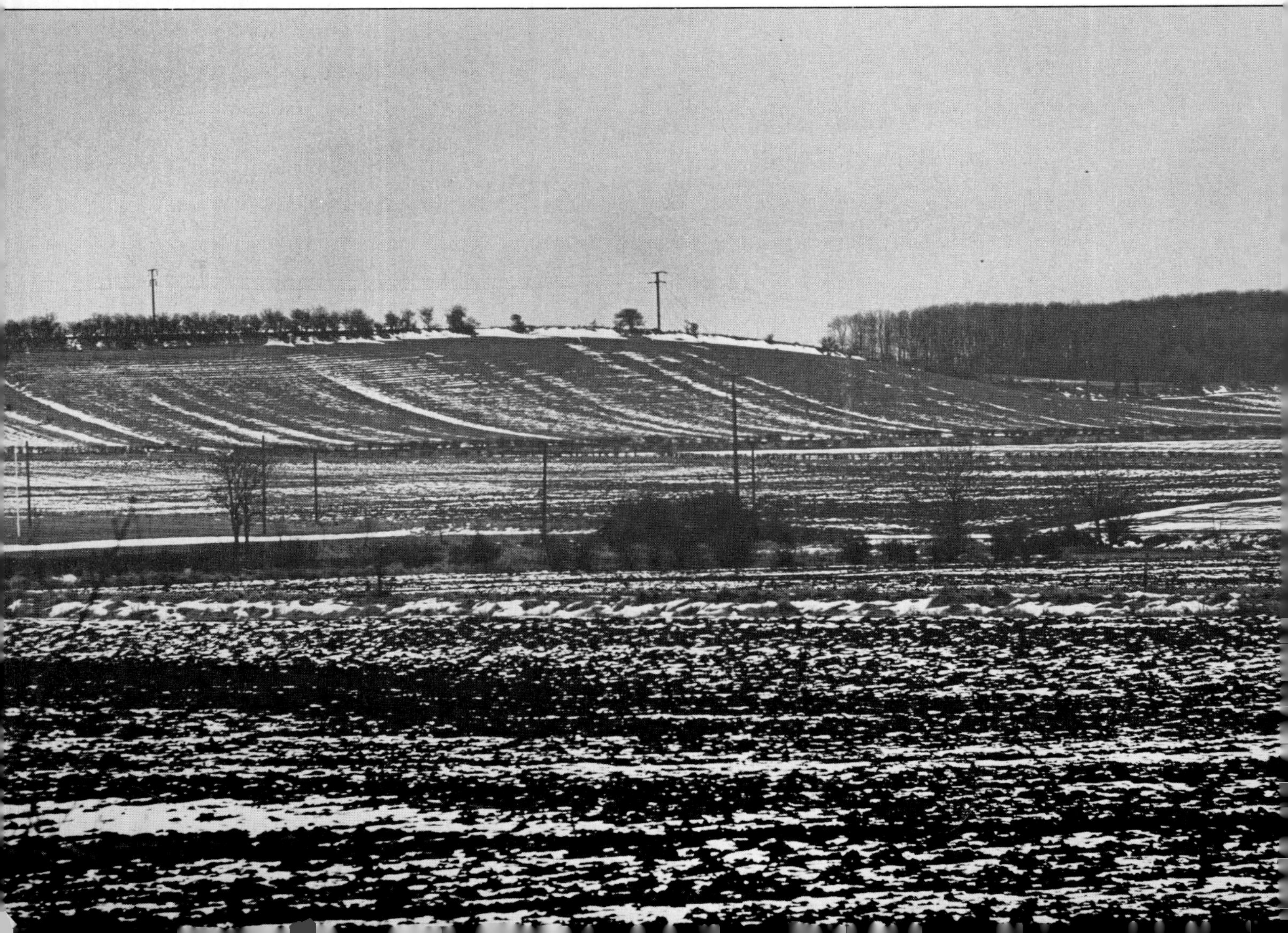

Victorian forbear and use a *tripod*; you will find that this also aids your composition.

An ideal way to present comparison pictures is as a series of slides dissolving into each other. Professional equipment for this can be purchased, but a simple hand-operated unit can be made quite cheaply from strong board. This is used with two matched projectors and one screen. Anyone who would like to follow this up should consult the many excellent books on *audio-visual* techniques.

Very useful sources of topographical pictures are the aerial photograph libraries. Cover varies, but every inch of the British Isles has been photographed vertically at least twice, once just after the war and again in the 1960s. However, obliques are more generally useful for our purposes and these can be purchased from the private companies specialising in this field like Aerofilms and Hunting Surveys. Alternatively, you can go out and take your own if you know an amateur flyer willing to pilot you around. Aerial photography is quite specialised and demands faultless camera technique with individual processing of the films to ensure adequate contrast. Archaeologists use air photographs a lot, and so, I suspect, would local historians if they understood better the technique and possibilities. Basic techniques are described in chapter eight.

Ancient features show in three different ways; as cropmarks, soilmarks and relief-marks. The aerial camera does not discriminate between historical periods, so that war time dispersals and searchlight sites can easily be confused with barrow cemeteries of the Bronze Age. Even an experienced interpreter of air pictures can sometimes be fooled, as when the present writer mistook a disused sewage farm for a barrow cemetery! Such incidents are, understandably, hard to live down.

Unfortunately most archaeology text-books give no details on how to take pictures, concentrating more on the finer points of interpretation. In this field, as in many others, no amount of book learning can substitute for practical experience, both in the air and on the ground.

Assuming that good aerial pictures have been obtained, the next step is to look at them carefully, preferably in the company of an expert from the nearest Archaeology Unit to help at first. Areas of interest can be noted on the two and a half inch map for further investigation. Archive research might suggest a deserted mediaval village. Are there any signs on the aerial pictures? What about the mediaeval field-system? Sometimes this latter can be almost entirely reconstructed from a good high altitude vertical taken in January. Be very careful with your interpretations. Genuine ridge and furrow nearly always displays an elongated reversed S curve. Straight ridge and furrow is possible, but is more likely to be land reclamation after open cast mining! Abandoned mineral lines may, after a few years, look remarkably like mediaeval

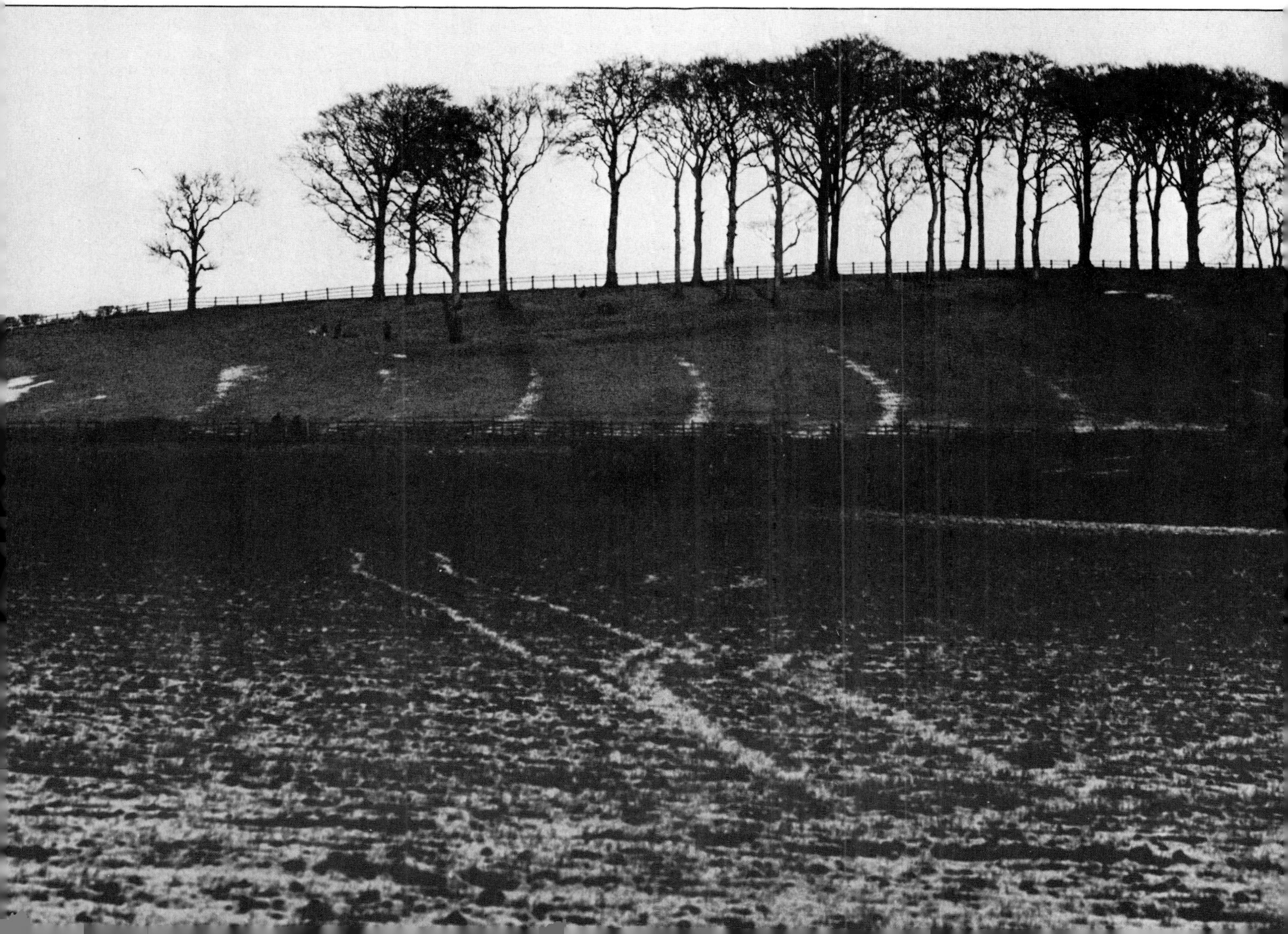

8. The ridge and furrow described in the text. Note that, though the mediaeval strips obviously extended towards the camera, agricultural activity has destroyed all traces. Carleton (W Yorks).

Minolta SR1v. 55mm lens. 1/30 at f1.7. Ilford FP4. A hand-held exposure at the very limit. Out of five negatives, only one was sharp.

hollow-ways, whilst natural gas pipelines are still occasionally mistaken for Roman roads! **Always** seek expert opinion before rushing into print.

The phenomena which we look for on aerial photographs are sometimes faintly visible to the ground observer, especially if he/she can climb something like a railway embankment or even on the roof of a vehicle. It is not generally realised that these manifestations can be outlined by other natural phenomena too, which make them easier to photograph especially on the ground. My own example occurred in 1978....

It was a very cold day in winter. Light snow was on the ground. During the mid-afternoon a light breeze sprang up which had the effect of melting the snow in exposed areas but leaving the sheltered places still white. Returning home early from work on foot, I glanced at 'The Rookeries', a picturesque avenue of trees in the village. There, outlined in white and green were the actual mediaeval strips which, presumably, no modern living person had seen before, or, more likely, recognised for what they were. The light was fading very quickly so I ran home, grabbed my cameras, and was just in time to photograph the scene before the light disappeared.

The land in question has since been ploughed and, needless to say, the strips have never again appeared despite visits at all times and seasons and even experiments with infra-red films.

Many years ago, when working as a milk-boy, I once saw a Civil War siege-work outlined in similar fashion, but of course had no camera available. In the Somme valley Roger Agache records Gallo-Roman sites from the air using the same phenomenon of differential melting, but of frost, whilst in the USA American airborn historians have noticed that floodwaters sometimes outline faint relief features.

When faced with anything of this nature any photograph is better than none. Whatever film is in your camera must suffice. If there is time to choose, a monochrome film will give your record a longer archival life and a better chance of publication. Needless to say, the marks, whatever they are, should be transcribed on a map as soon as possible. During this process small details like the curvature of lanes and boundaries, previously unremarked, may suggest the further extent of your feature.

The final record is really more a matter of cartography rather than photography, and ideally should take the form of a series of map overlays showing the same landscape at different periods, all superimposed on the natural features. This can form the basis of a fascinating illustrated talk using dissolve projection, or perhaps a two screen presentation showing slides of the maps and the actual features together.

During your research do not neglect to show people at work. These pictures become part of the history of your local history! Shots of individuals dating hedges, field-walking, etc., all add interest for your eventual audience - the interested general public.

When everything is polished and complete, consider having a video recording made to lodge in the local museum or library. This could, perhaps, be loaned to interested organisations and form a useful earner of donations, as well as spreading interest and free publicity about the society.

9. A long telephoto shot, taken in appalling conditions, showing how thin, windblown snow reveals both mediaeval ridge and furrow and also a possible Civil War siege work on the hill slopes, centre. Pontefract (W Yorks).

Minolta SR1v. 135mm lens plus 2X Teleconverter (effectively 270mm) Tripod. Ilford HP5.

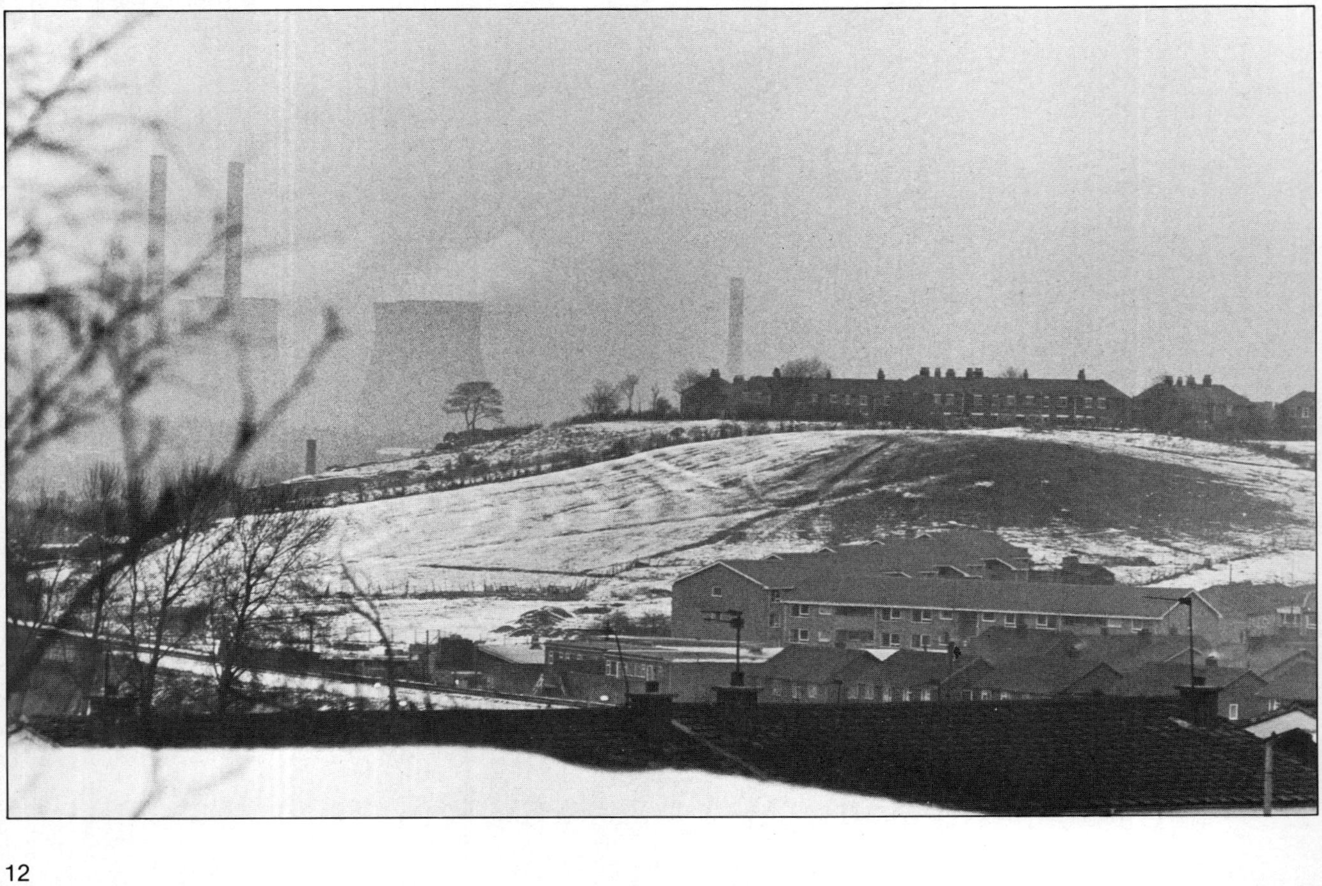

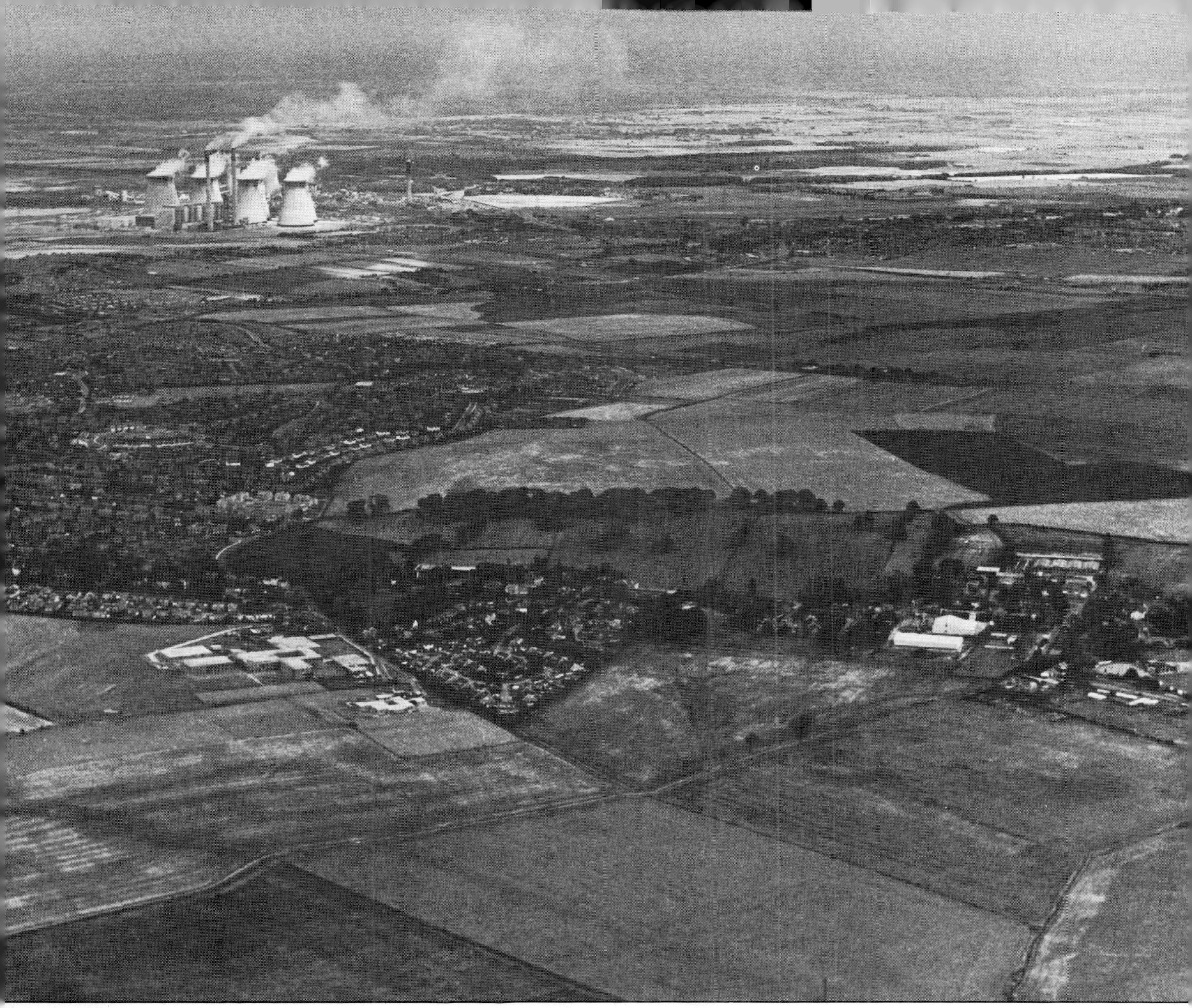

10. A high-oblique taken from 4,500 feet at the end of July 1978. Not only does this show the present landscape, but also several clues to past landscapes: near the bottom left corner can be seen crop marks of mediaeval ridge and furrow. Near the centre, the kite shaped field has a series of nineteenth century ornamental ponds beneath it. Modern attempts to drain the marshy centre of the field are clear. Immediately beyond the avenue of trees (centre) is a clear crop mark of a prehistoric 'banjo' site.

Minolta SR1v. 55mm lens. Kodak Plus X, processed for contrast after exposure through an orange filter.

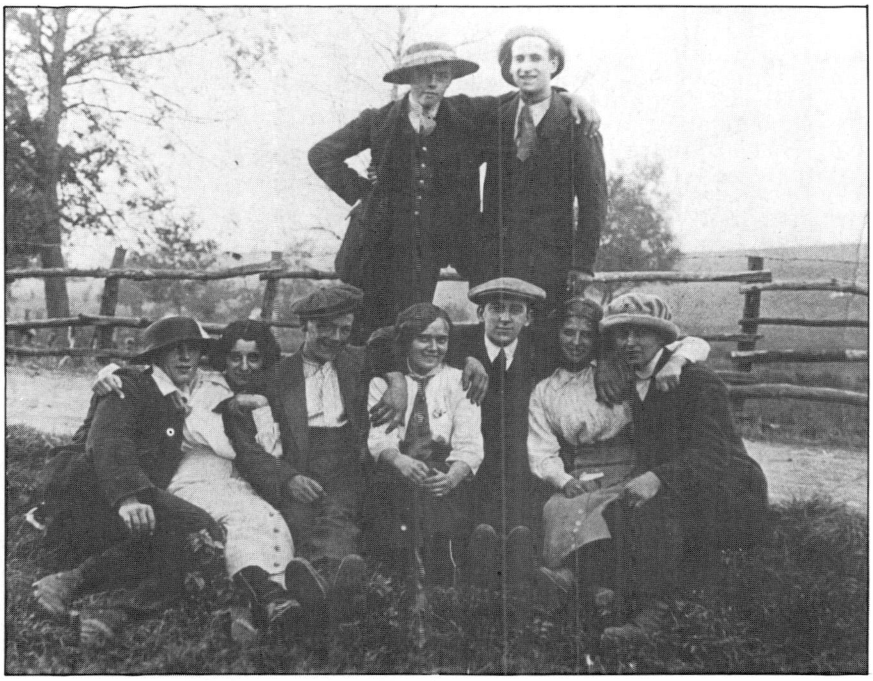

11. A group snapshot from about the time of the Great War. This was obviously taken by an experienced worker, as the quality is excellent, in spite of the obvious losses due to copying, mechanical damage and reproduction. Though not taken as a landscape picture, such snapshots can provide useful landscape data, as the fashions allow close dating.

Copy made with 35mm Minolta SLR, 55mm lens, Ilford FP4.

CHAPTER THREE

Recording Buildings

'The systematic study of the houses of a parish, a town, or a region, will tell us a great deal that is nowhere recorded in documents. Yet few local historians have attempted this task, partly because they are still blind to the high value of visual evidence and partly because if they are aware of the existence of this evidence, they feel it is beyond their powers and knowledge.'

The extract above is from the introduction to chapter six of Professor Hoskin's book, *Fieldwork in Local History*. Twenty years after he wrote these words they are still apposite. Soon after the book first appeared the present writer and his colleagues in the Pontefract and District Archaeological Society began a systematic street by street photographic record of their town. It was not a minute too soon, as the 'developers' moved in shortly afterwards and many fine old buildings were replaced by characterless monstrosities.

One of the problems is, of course, that buildings are deceptively permanent; so much so that the local history photographer is tempted to keep putting off recording them, until they suddenly disappear. I refer, of course, to the ordinary, hardly notable houses, shops, pubs, etc. that fill our towns and villages. The well known historic buildings are a different case and should have been recorded long since by the National Monuments Record, the County Archaeological Unit, or the local museum. It is the so-called ordinary ones which provide the shocks. For example, a short time ago consent was given to alter a timber-framed shop in the centre of Pontefract. At the same time the row of undistinguished 'Victorian' workshops behind it were to be demolished. Though these latter had been photographed in the extensive programme of the late sixties, their exteriors were again recorded and their extensive cellars, entered via the shop-front, were also drawn and recorded. Access to the workshops was not obtained, or even thought necessary. When actual demolition began, however, it was discovered that the workshops were in fact timber-framed mediaeval buildings which had been given the air of uniformity with a brick 'skin', new windows and doors. Luckily, most of the important information about them was obtained one Sunday

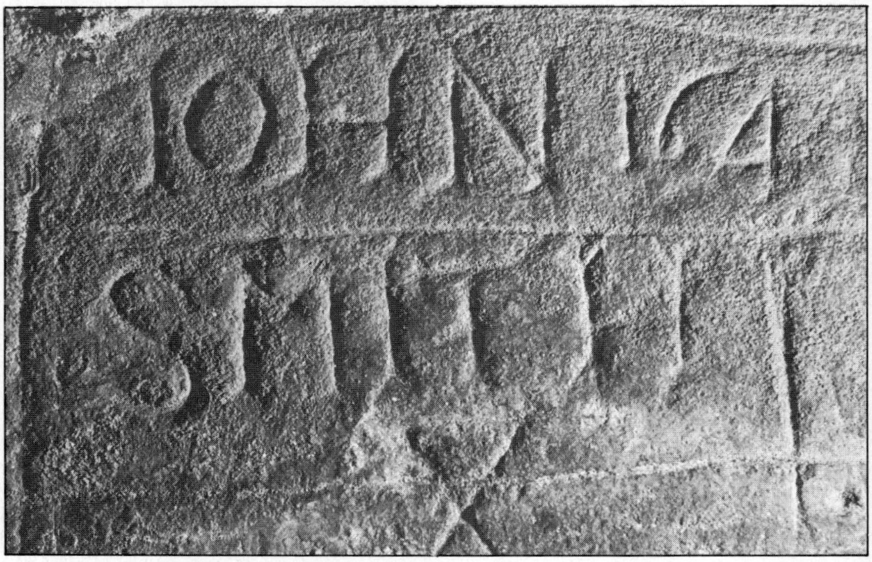

12. One of the prisoner's names in the dungeons at Pontefract Castle, photographed using the rig illustrated in plate 15.

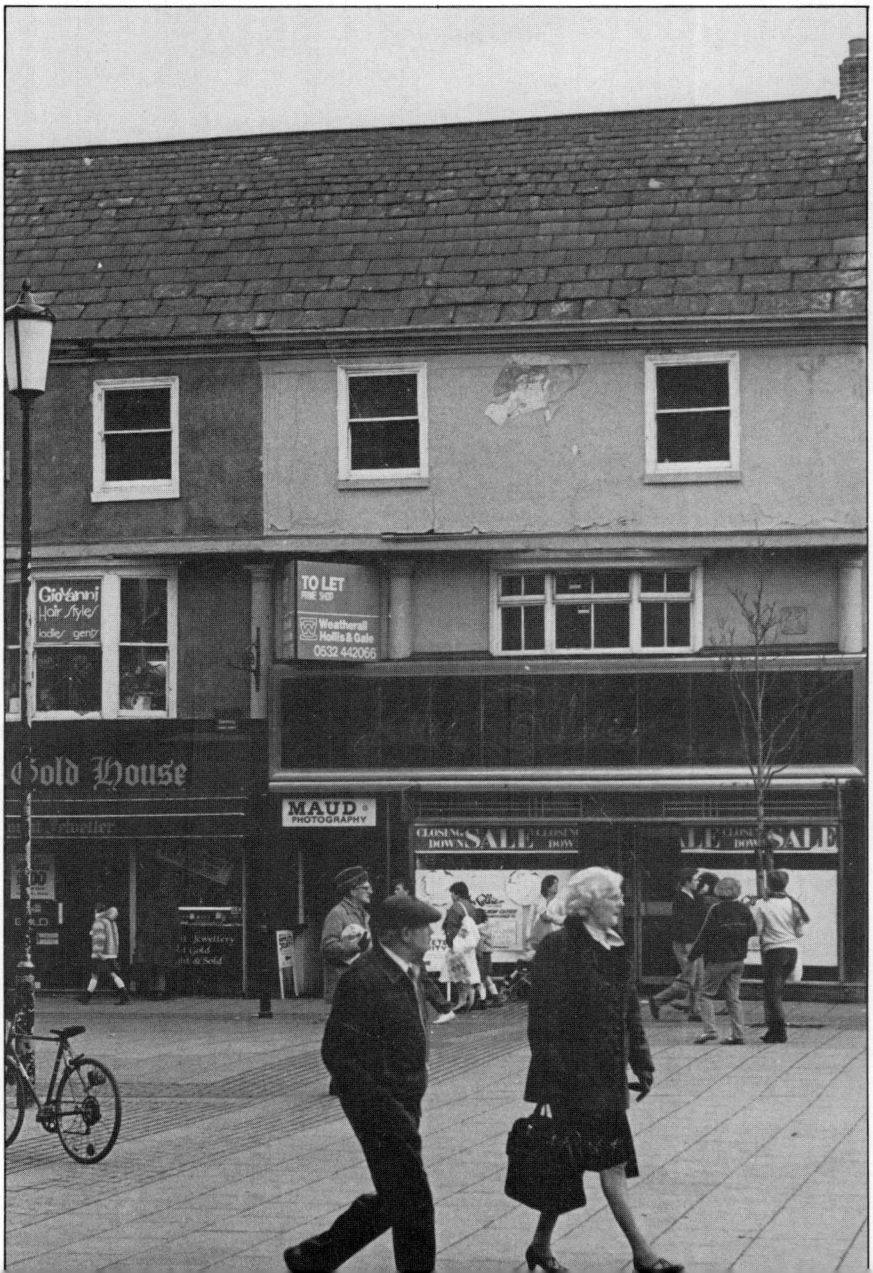

13. 55mm lens for an almost straight-on exterior view. Though the pedestrians do not obtrude and hide nothing of the building, they provide useful dating evidence.

morning when access and visibility were improved by partial demolition.

This situation is not uncommon in our older towns, and calls for constant vigilance. As photographers, we tend to forget the importance of other forms of recording. Plans, sketches and notes are of equal or greater value and take longer to complete. Thus, when working out how long it is going to take to record a particular building, time must be allowed for these other activities. If a bulldozer is in the offing and there is no time at all, photography becomes the only viable recording system and everything else must be subordinated to it. It is quite possible to extrapolate measurements from photographs and a number of universities have computerised machines which can do this. Those people with a mathematical turn of mind can actually do the calculations themselves, see Williams, *Simple Photogrammetry.*

The first chapter dealt quite comprehensively with the 35mm SLR. This is the ideal type of camera for undertaking building record work with, but there are other types which will do almost as good a job. Of these, the most common is the *35mm compact*, an instrument which lives up to its name in being very compact and pocketable. Modern examples of the type have so many automated functions that the user has little to think about. Loading, film-transport, focusing, exposure and re-winding are all taken care of. Many have an integral flash unit which charges and fires automatically when the light level drops. Whatever instrument is used, the most vital piece of equipment is between the photographer's ears, ie a knowledge of technique, lighting, film and instrument capability, etc. Having stated this, I now prefer to work with a fairly comprehensive outfit which (so far) has proved itself the equal of every photographic situation, from building record to aerial work. It consists of two SLR bodies, one each for mono and colour, with 28mm, 35 to 70mm zoom and 80 to 200mm zoom. The outfit is completed with several powerful flashguns, including an ancient bulb gun originally purchased at a jumble sale for twenty five pence. When used with the bigger flashbulbs, now increasingly difficult to find, it gives much more light than even the most powerful electronic unit. Other equipment includes *slaves* (light activated triggers which remove the need to trail cables between flashguns), *filters* and spare battery packs. These latter tend to be forgotten, but are every bit as important as the camera! After several nasty experiences of batteries dying on a Sunday evening, I now use *Nicad* re-chargeable batteries and always keep a spare pack of four fully charged.

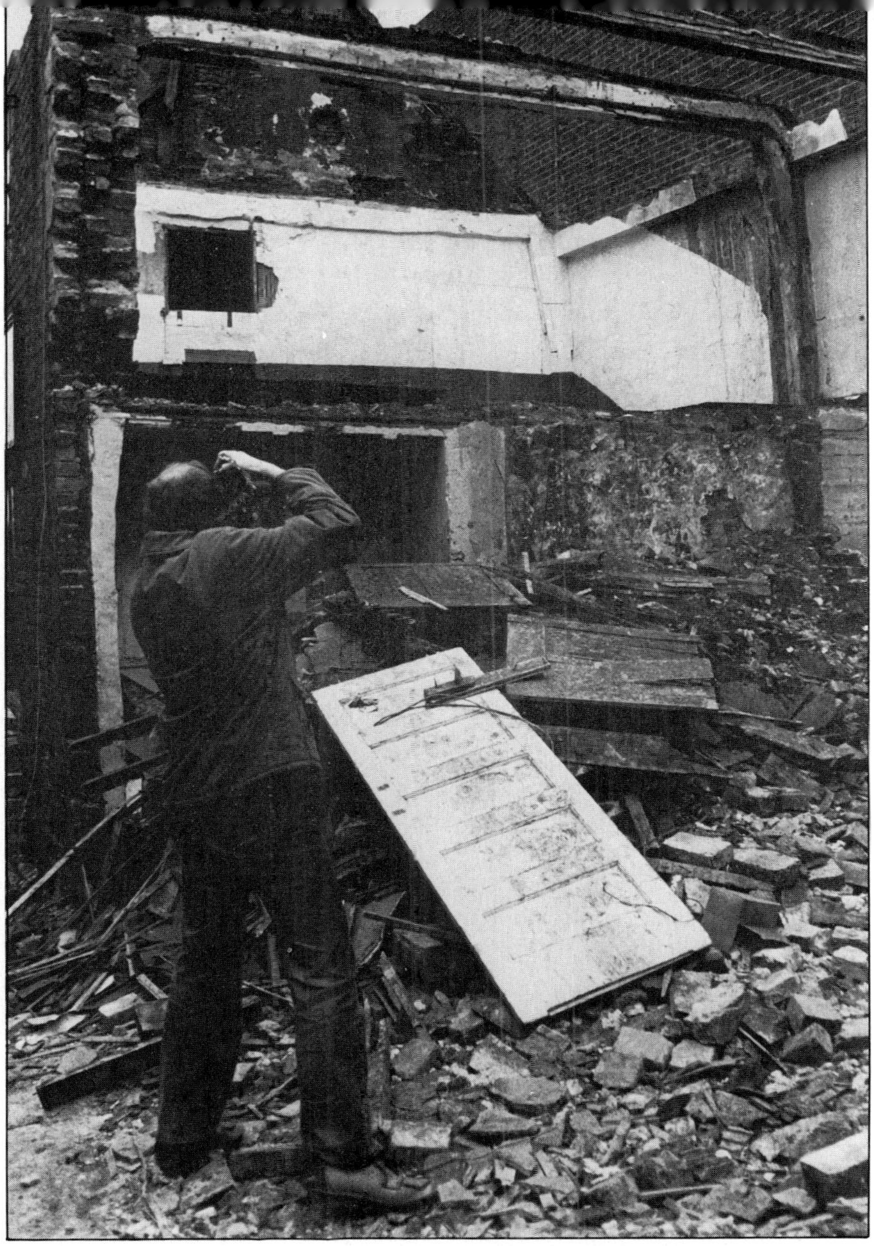

14. A zoom lens is useful to pick out important details from a distance.

A strong case or bag is important. Old buildings tend to have a lot of dust and during demolition, or even alteration, this flies all over. Dust is one of the worst enemies of precision equipment and does not do electronic circuits much good either.

Of the lenses, the 28mm is useful in a confined space. 35mm is an excellent focal length for building records, whilst telephotos and the longer end of zooms can be used to pick out distant detail like chimneys, guttering, inscriptions etc.

Filters are sheets of optical glass or resin, used chiefly to alter the response of monochrome film to light. They normally have little use in building records but can occasionally prove invaluable. Ordinary red brick takes on an exciting but not inaccurate tone when shot through an orange filter. Filters really come into their own when something like wall-paintings are discovered. Say, for example, you found an interior wall covered in a rare type of mediaeval mural painting. The colours are very basic, being blue and red on a white ground. Unfortunately blue and the red are both the same tone in black and white, so some method of differentiation is necessary. The answer is to use a filter, remembering the rule that any colour will lighten its own and darken opposites. Therefore by using a red or orange filter reds will be lightened and the blues darkened, whilst the converse applies to a blue filter which lightens blues and darkens reds. Some exposure increase is necessary with a filter fitted and this must be calculated carefully, as over-exposure nullifies the effect.

Film used will vary with the lighting and the time of year. My own preferences are for Ilford FP4 in summer and HP5 in winter. For colour I like Fujichrome professional films, using 100 RDP in summer and 400 RDP in winter. It must be emphasised that all the major brands are good today and I would be equally happy using equivalent emulsions from any of them.

Of course, photography is only half the record. A knowledge of vernacular building is important or significant details can be missed. Often this can be picked up from older or more experienced members of the recording team, but judicious reading also helps.

Another vital aspect which cannot be ignored is simply gaining access to the building. The best time is probably just before demolition or alteration, as bits of plaster can be pulled off, panelling removed, etc. Permission is, of course, necessary, and there are two approaches. The correct way is to write to the company which owns the property. This takes time, and the person who eventually answers the letter will be familiar with all the regulations and insurance requirements, and is therefore quite likely to refuse! A better approach is to ask the senior person on the spot, the demolition foreman, who will usually agree.

Always remember that old buildings and demolition sites are dangerous. Wear a safety helmet if possible and old but serviceable clothes. Footware is important; rusty nails abound and will penetrate easily 'town' type shoes. Good boots or strong shoes are probably best, though the reinforced wellingtons supplied by British Coal and other heavy industries have proved their worth. If your group also excavates, then all the active members will be up to date with their anti-tetanus injections, or should be, but if not do not neglect this vital precaution. Group insurance is also a wise investment.

Actual photography must begin before demolition. Good views of all exterior walls are important, preferably taken from a viewpoint directly opposite and about half as high as the building. This is not always possible and some oblique shooting may be necessary. Often important detail can be obscured by parked vehicles or even masses of pedestrians. In this situation you must go early on a Sunday morning, unless the building is next to a church! The rule regarding lenses is exactly the same as for shooting archaeological earth sections, and for the same purpose - to avoid distortion. Always use the longest focal length lens which will cover the subject, though on the ground this may mean a 35mm or even a 24mm wide-angle. With any lens it is important to avoid tilting the camera upwards, otherwise you might get converging verticles, where the sides of buildings appear to converge instead of appearing parallel. Complete the exterior by picking out important detail with a telephoto or the long end of a zoom.

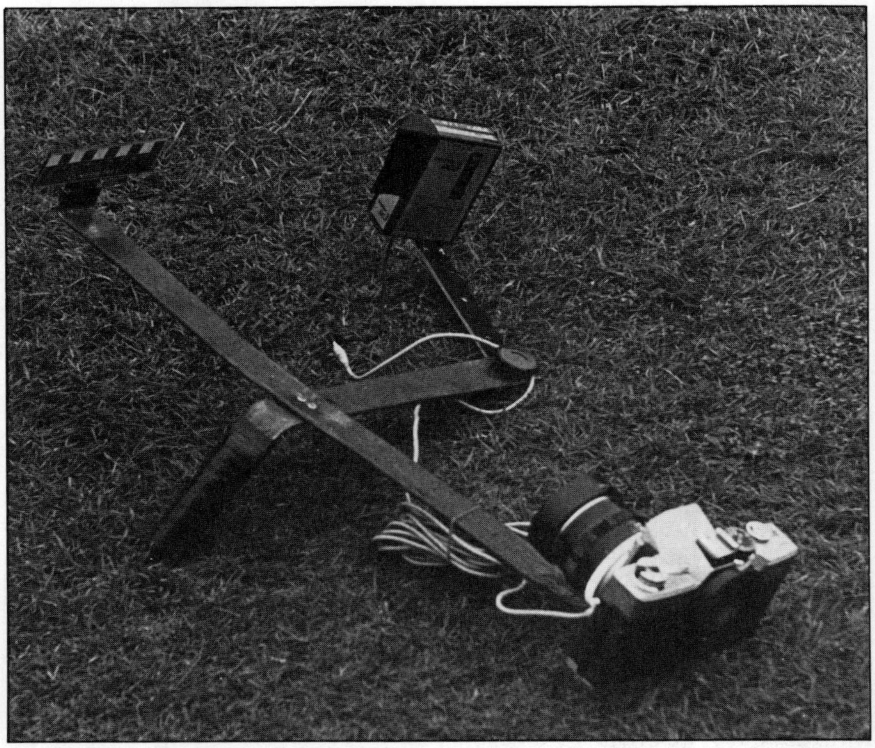

15. The special rig designed to record large numbers of graffiti in a short time.

One aspect of exteriors which causes problems is the ubiquitous cement rendering. More than once has a rendered house been demolished, and only at this stage is it noticed that the rendering is part of a comparatively recent modernisation, and that the house was a timber-framed mediaeval or Tudor building. Now there is a way to see through old rendering. Unfortunately, it does not work on new or freshly painted cement, but as techniques become refined perhaps soon even this will be possible. The film to use is *Kodak High Speed Infra-red Film 2481*. This must be ordered from a Kodak dealer, as it cannot be bought over the counter. Special precautions are needed, both for loading and unloading the camera and for developing, chiefly because many cameras and even darkroom blackout materials are transparent to infra-red light. Practice loading the camera in the dark before actually doing it with the IR film. Load at night and in an interior room with no external doors or windows. Use an old, all metal-bodied camera with a lens marked for IR focusing (this is usually a red bar on the focusing scale next to the normal centre mark). A deep red filter must be fitted to the lens, and an efficient lens hood is advised. Most exposure meters do not measure infra-red rays, but a *hand-held meter* set for 100 ISO usually suffices. Photography is best undertaken in bright sunlight as this is rich in IR. Bracket exposures by a stop either way, ie if the meter says 1/125th at f8, shoot pictures at the same speed, but at f5.6 and f11 as well as at f8. Take the readings from the actual building, angling the meter to avoid reading from the sky. Before shooting, focus carefully and then move the indicated distance to the IR focusing mark. Develop carefully following Kodak's instructions to the letter. I first tried this film for urban recording three years ago, and in one afternoon discovered three timber-framed buildings!

Interiors are more difficult to picture than exteriors, except during demolition, when the absence of a roof gives more light. Normally, each room must be carefully lit with multiple lights and the exposure made from a tripod. In thirty years I have never yet managed to find time to approach this ideal. Usually it is a matter of substituting volume of lighting for quality; that is, a big flash on a hand-held camera. A wide-angle lens makes it possible to cover each room in two shots. At one time when doing this I moved members of the recording team out of shot, but recently have started leaving them in the pictures, for two reasons; one, to act as scales and two, to provide built-in dating evidence on the photograph. The main flash is a powerful unit which is sometimes helped by one of less power. In this situation the main flash is held to one side by a helper and the other is on the camera. A *slave*, attached to the main unit, fires it in response to the burst of light from the unit on the camera. It is most important to avoid shooting when there is dust in the air, as this only reflects the light straight back into the lens, fogging the picture. If necessary sit down and wait for the dust to clear.

Complete the interior pictures by looking for details like panelling, painted plaster, chimney-pieces, etc. Low-relief subjects like mason's marks and graffiti need a special technique. The flat lighting produced by camera-mounted flash causes them, in effect, to disappear. The remedy for this situation is to use very oblique lighting, ie light from an acute side-angle. If there are just a few low relief subjects the necessary side light can be provided by a colleague with a hand-held flash to one side on an extension cable, or with a slave fitted. When there are a lot to be photographed this method proves to be too laborious, as I found when trying to record the seventeenth century graffiti in the dungeon at Pontefract Castle. I solved the problem by building a special rig from scrap steel. This enabled one person to take all the pictures very quickly and efficiently. The rig is illustrated in Plate 6.

Non-photographic accessories for interiors include a whisk-brush for removing dust, a piece of chalk to emphasize detail, and a ten centimetre scale.

I took my first building-record photographs thirty years ago. Luckily the prints are still in good condition, luckily because after the local photographer printed them for me (this was before I set up my own darkroom) the family dog chewed the negatives. Copy prints are of course possible but can never reproduce the subtlety of tone and detail on a good negative. Ever after that I filed my negatives very carefully indeed.

Another interesting omission from those old pictures is people. Obviously, pure record photographs do not need figures, but nowadays I always make a point of including a few shots of the recording team at work. Not only are such pictures useful for illustrating lectures and even books. Eventually they become part of the history of your society.

16. Wide angle lens (in this case a 28mm) and powerful flash in combination enable a good record to be made, even in the cramped confines of a wheelhouse.

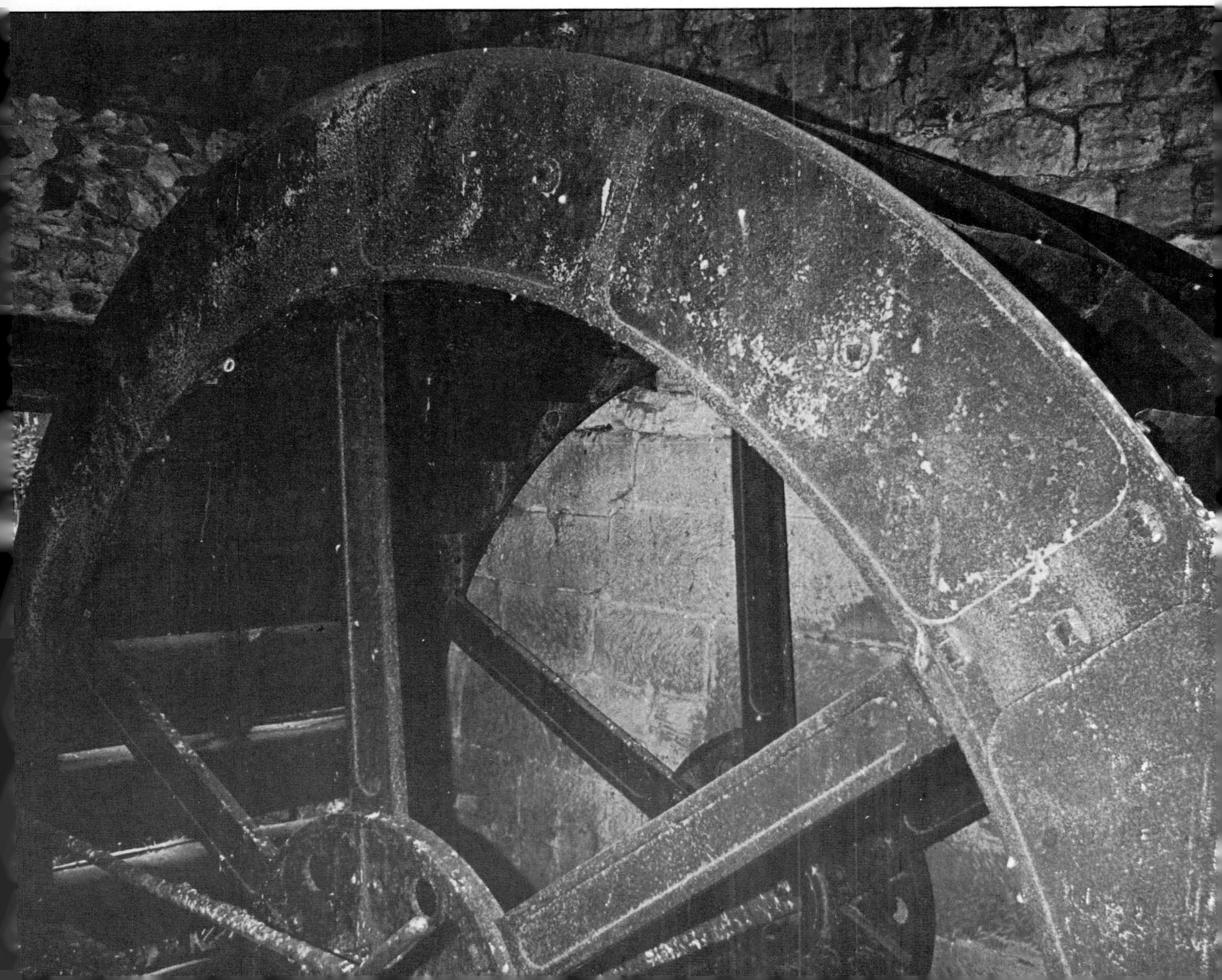

CHAPTER FOUR

People for Posterity

People like pictures of other people. Old group pictures draw large crowds at local history expositions, and the family historian now makes increasing use of photographs. Luckily our ancestors have left us large numbers of pictures of all kinds documenting their activities. This chapter will show how you can carry on the tradition, giving your counterpart of the future a pictorial record of family, friends, workmates and the community.

Photography has been around since the late 1830s. Though the majority of the images made have been destroyed (deliberately, accidently, by enemy action or decay) sufficient survive to give us a good idea of what people looked like, what they enjoyed doing and where they went. The modern photographer, with intentions of adding to that record, could usefully make a close study of old photographs, both to emulate his/her counterpart and, more importantly, to identify gaps where propriety, technology or economic conditions have made the record incomplete. For example, there are few good indoor photographs of dinners, presentations, parties, etc. before the 1930s. This is probably because the means of obtaining such pictures was primitive, dangerous and dirty; I refer, of course, to the use of flashpowder, a semi-explosive mixture which was ignited by a variety of devices of doubtful reliability. The powder itself had to be carefully measured, and ignition had to be timed to occur when the shutter of the camera was open. Following the ignition and the (hoped for) flash, the photographer had to beat a hasty retreat before the noxious combustion-products settled over the subject of the picture! The foil-filled flashbulb was introduced in the 1930s, and its successor, electronic flash, gradually took over from the late 1940s.

17. The craftsman brushmaker described in the text. One of a series taken with direct flash. We had a cassette recorder running as we spoke to him and took the pictures.

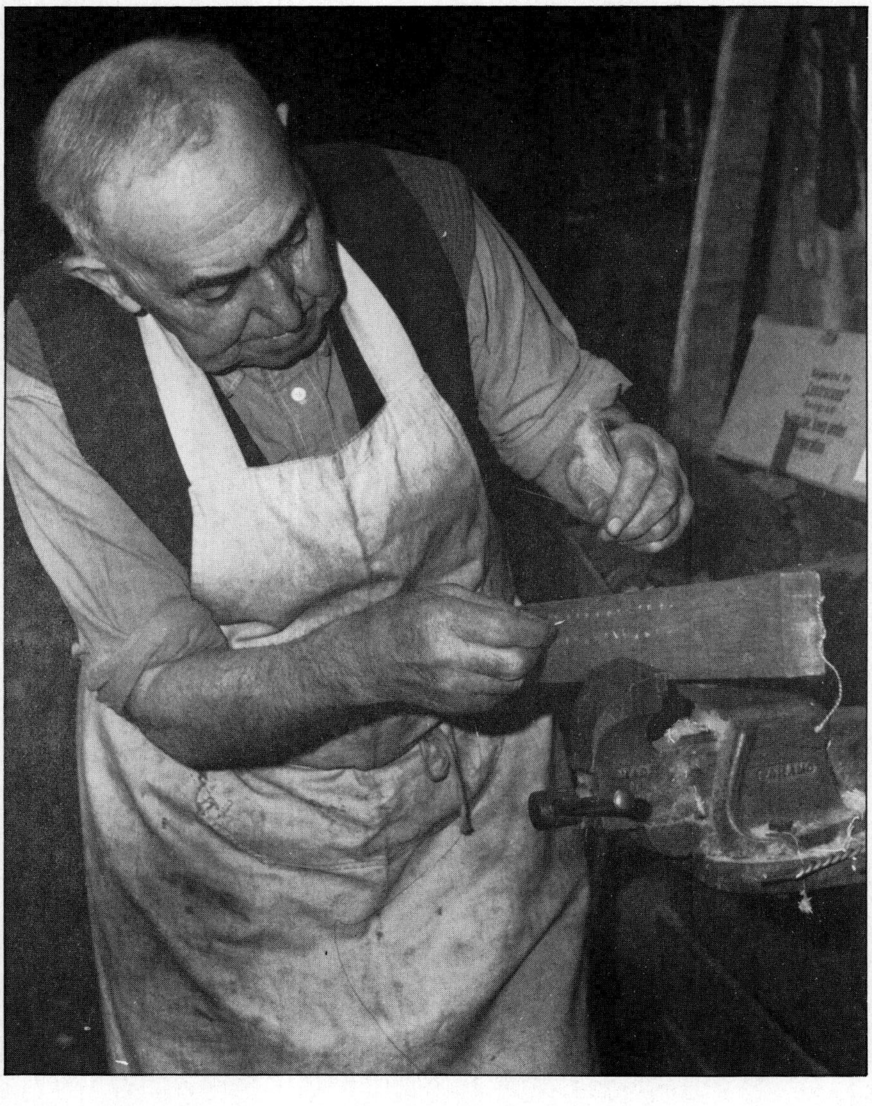

Another gap is the one caused by economic conditions. Most early pictures tend to be of upper or middle class groups, simply because they were the people who could afford to commission a photographer or buy a camera. By the twenties snaps of working-class origin became more common but, again, indoor pictures lag behind because of the complications of the flashpowder and, later, the expense of flashbulbs.

Today photography is comparatively cheap and most families own at least one good camera. In real terms both equipment and materials have fallen in price, whilst the increased use of high technology has made it possible to obtain perfect exposure and even focus in almost any situation.

Let us assume then, that you are about to begin a photographic record of the people in your town, city or village. Your first consideration will be what equipment and materials to use. If you have followed my advice in the earlier chapters you will probably already have a 35mm SLR or a 35mm compact, or be contemplating the purchase of one. Both are excellent tools for people-pictures, each having its own advantages. With a single lens reflex, the ideal lens is a wide to normal zoom, something in the region of 28mm to 70mm. The compact is already fitted with one moderate wide angle lens (usually about 38mm) and some also have the option of a short telephoto. For *prime lens* enthusiasts (a prime lens is one of single, fixed, focal length, ie not a zoom), the best lens would be one slightly wider than normal; say 35mm or thereabouts. This focal length, once the standard of pressmen, has gone out of favour recently, and the dealers' shelves are groaning with good second-hand examples at ridiculously low prices. Not long since one of my favourite dealers in Leeds sold off a whole batch of good 35mm lenses, f2.8, fully automatic diaphragm (all modern SLR lenses are FAD. This means that after viewfinding through the taking lens at full aperture, the lens is automatically stopped down to the taking aperture as you press the release), for £10 each! One of the unsung advantages of the 35mm lens is that this focal length is the widest that the average flashgun can cover without special attachments. In addition, being a wide angle, it has the advantage, common to all its species, of needing less care with its focussing.

When considering which film to

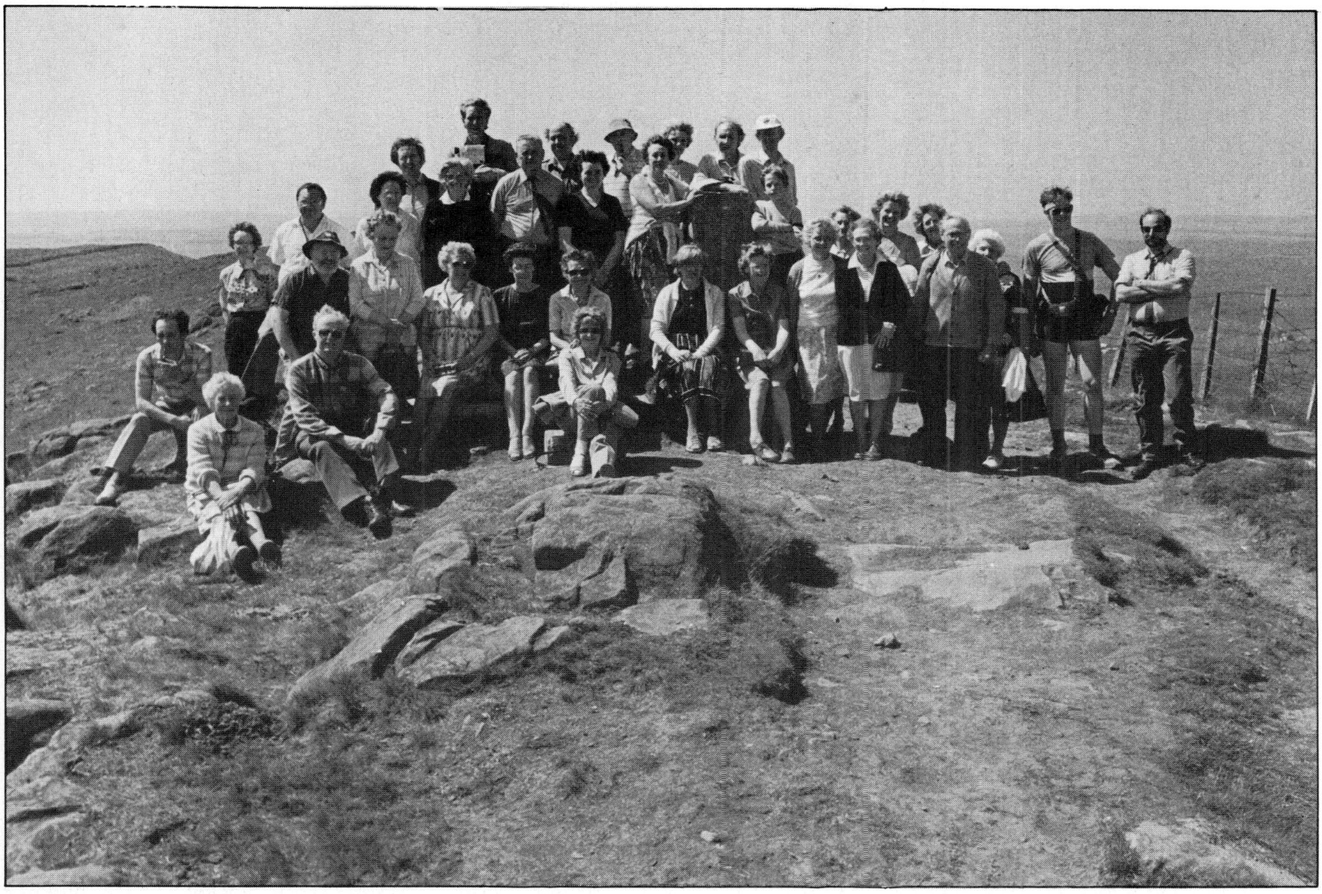

use, please bear in mind the advantages of monochrome stock outlined in chapter one. Unfortunately relatives, thinking only of the present, prefer colour, so some compromise has to be reached. One method is to shoot on colour negative stock and have the film processed and printed commercially. The best negatives are then enlarged onto monochrome paper and processed for permanence. There is, naturally, a drop in quality, but colour films are improving quickly, so eventually there should be little difference. Another compromise which I often adopt is to shoot on colour reversal film, for transparencies, and then print selected pictures onto *Cibachrome*.

In your study of early photographs you will have noticed that the formal family group has fallen from fashion in the last few decades. This is a great loss, especially to family historians who will feel the deprivation more towards the end of the century and beyond. Ideally you should remedy the situation by visiting a professional photographer who will always make a better job than an amateur. If you must take the picture yourself, using the self-timer to trip the camera, bear these hints in mind:

1) Arrange your sitters in such a way that their heads are on different levels;
2) Ensure that no feet, legs etc. stick too far out of the group or the picture area;
3) Bounce your flash from the (white) ceiling just in front of the group, or pose in good light and put the camera on a tripod;
4) Carefully identify and name each person on the back of each print, and date each picture. Use a proper pen for this. Many ordinary pens have ink with very low stability which can either fade quickly, or migrate through the print onto the picture surface.

General Outdoor Photography

Part of the pleasure of recording people is the opportunity which it gives to get out and about, and also the heightened awareness of what is going on around you, which the act of photography seems to bring out. Try this useful exercise: load your camera with a monochrome film appropriate for the season, ie 125 ISO for summer or 400 ISO for winter. Go and visit your local market. Find a good vantage point and just stand and watch what is going on. Eventually, start taking pictures. You will probably find that you feel a little embarrassed using a camera when not on holiday! This will soon pass. With posterity in mind, try to include prominent buildings in the background. Permanent structures, like churches and market halls, are ideal. Try taking long-shots and close-ups of people buying and selling, chatting, eating etc. These are probably best taken with a *telephoto lens* (one of the longer than normal focal length) or the longer end of a zoom. After processing carefully caption and date each picture. Repeat the whole exercise at different seasons of the year.

18. Members and friends of the Pontefract & District Archaeological Society pose around the Triangulation Point at Winshields, on Hadrian's Wall, Summer 1985.

Something else well worth recording is the special event. By this I mean fairs, pageants, historical centenaries etc. These tend to occur in summer so the light is usually good. For most events of this type a medium telephoto lens is best, an 80-200 zoom being my own choice. Again with posterity in mind, try to

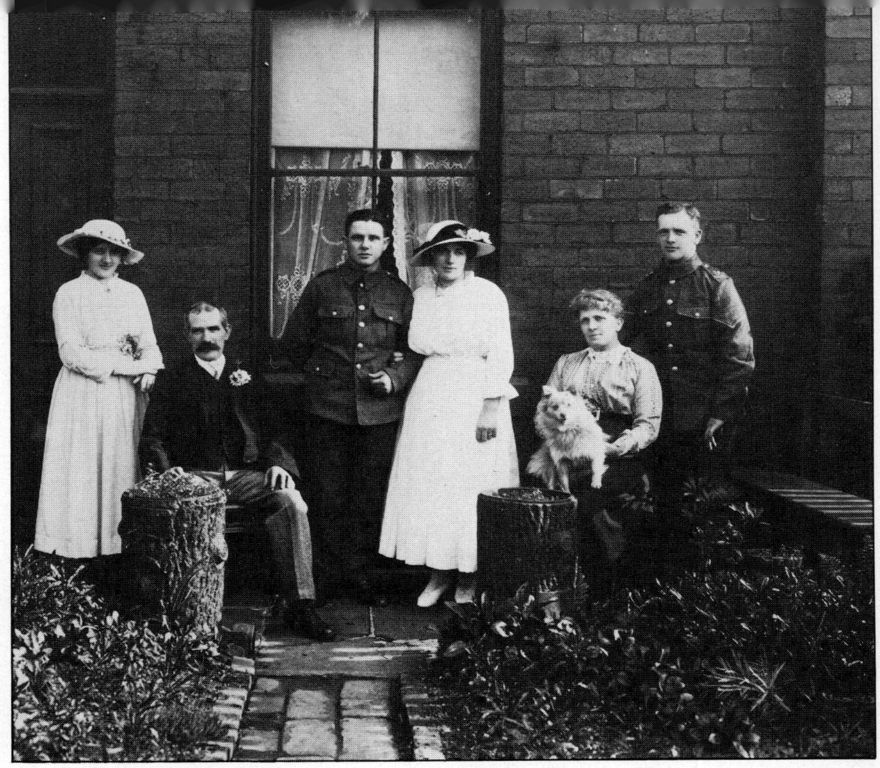

20. Weddings provide good opportunities to snap family groups. This group is doubly valuable, as it is posed in front of the family home - note the Victorian water softeners in use as flower pots!

choose backgrounds carefully, setting the scene so that your successors can identify the place and the event. Examine the picture of the street entertainers, Plate 4. The viewpoint was chosen extremely carefully, framing with the zoom so that the bunting across the road and the town hall in the background all contributed to the picture and set it firmly in space and time. A zoom is particularly useful for this sort of thing as by altering the focal length it is possible to alter the size of the background; in other words, referring to the same example, the town hall clock behind the crowd would appear twice as big at 200mm as it would at 100mm.

If you yourself are part of the action in an event such as this then a wide-angle lens, the short end of short zoom, or a compact camera, is best. With a 28mm lens set at f11 and the focussing set to eight feet, everything will be sharp from three and a half feet to infinity. This phenomena is called *depth of field*, and it can be deliberately controlled by the photographer once the basics are understood. Pictures shot from within the action using a compact or a wide angle lens often have an immediacy that others lack.

Have you ever considered photographing your work? Our crafts, trades and professions will be of immense interest in the future, so a film shot on the theme of a day at work would be a real investment. Our jobs vary so much that little advice can be given here, except to state the obvious to a readership of historians, that a good bright well-lit picture is worth any number of dark, moody, poorly-lit ones of the type favoured by the trendier photographic press. Some years ago I had the chance to take a definitive series of pictures of the last craftsman brushmaker at work in his dark, very 'atmospheric' workshop. I originally considered using very fast film without auxiliary lighting, but luckily realised that though such pictures might win competitions, they would be less useful as historical records. Accordingly, the pictures were taken on slow film using camera-mounted flash. Though hardly pretty, they are quite useful, as they show a lot of detail.

What about voluntary work? Much of this is never recorded so will hardly rate a mention in the history books. Another exercise which I once undertook was to accompany my wife when she delivered 'Meals on Wheels' to local pensioners. Though hardly spectacular as pictures, the shots form a useful record and were, in fact, published in the local paper.

National events having an impact at local level should not be neglected. During the recent miners' strike, a member of the local camera club took some superb pictures of the pickets relaxing outside the nearby colliery. Because the author was an

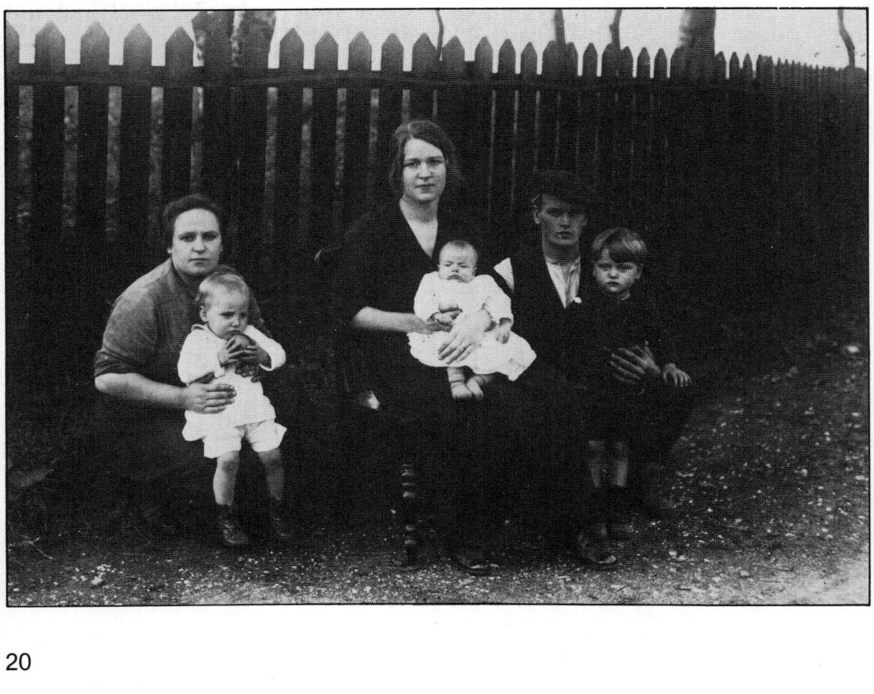

19. Why a professional photographer took this photograph will never be known, but he has provided us with a useful image of working class people which can be dated by reference to the clothing.

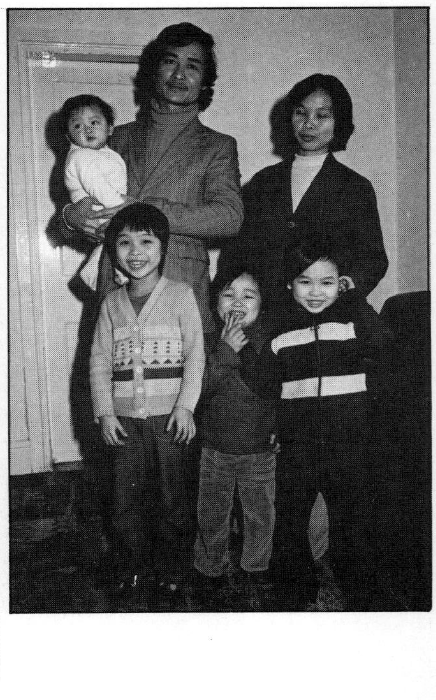

21. The Phi family, who (with other Vietnamese boat people) spent some time at a reception centre in Carleton. It is important for the local history photographer to record such groups passing through.

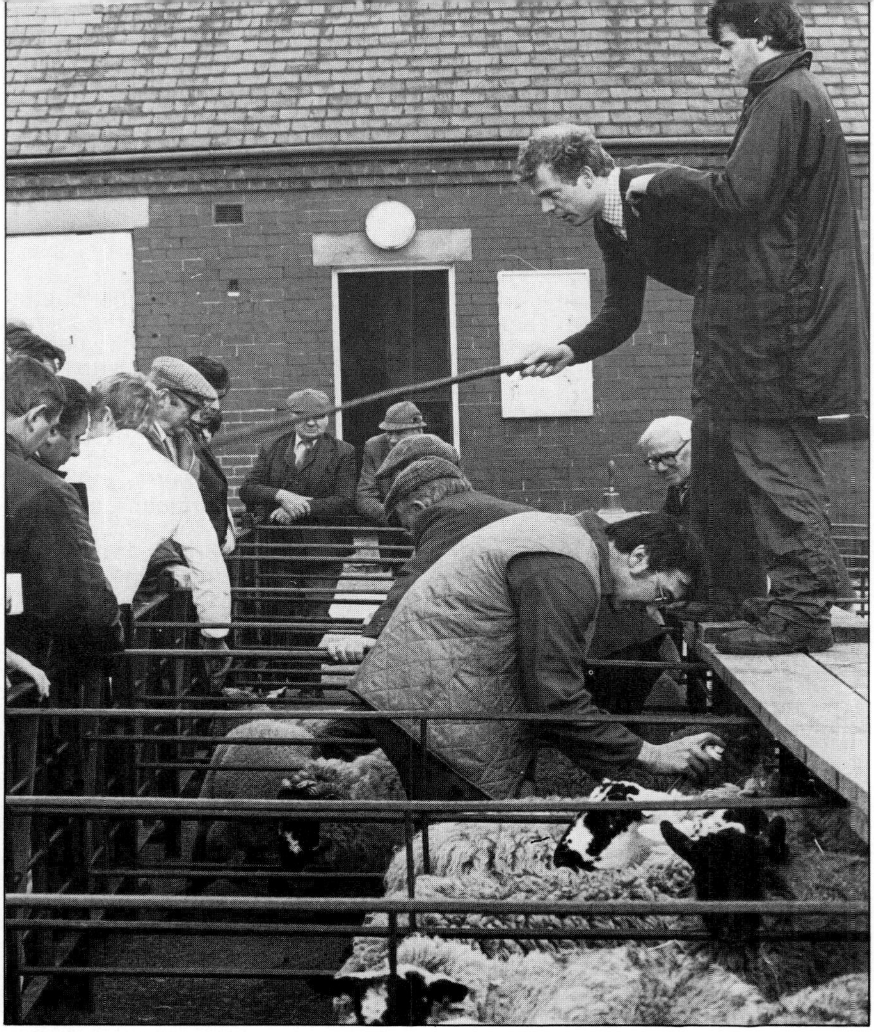

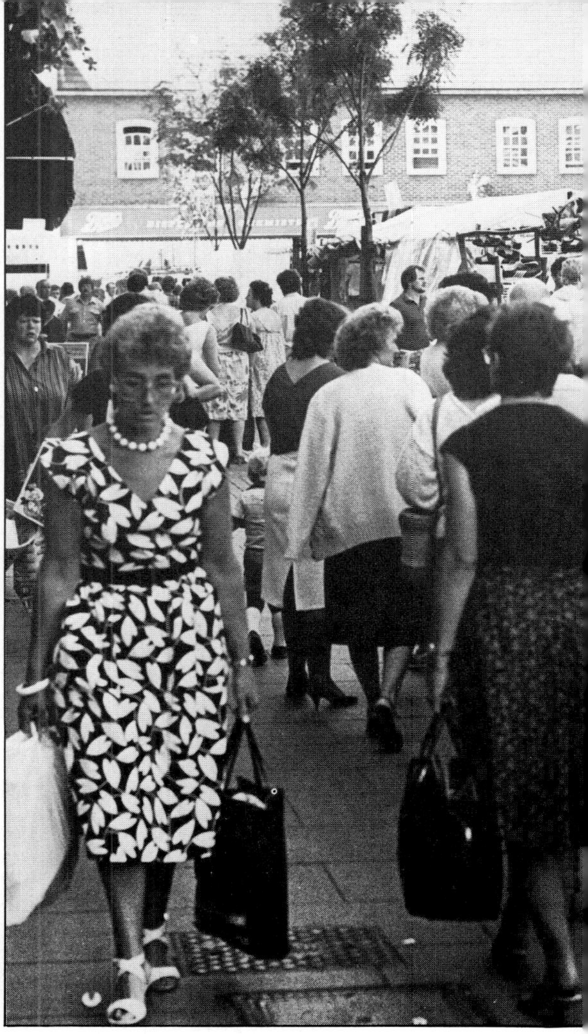

experienced (and talented) amateur photographer, the photographs were exceptionally good, showing plenty of detail but also very well composed. Whatever personal views may have been on the Scargill strike, pictures like this form a priceless record, and I urged the author to lodge copies in the town museum.

24. Making a museum inventory. Another society activity well worth recording.

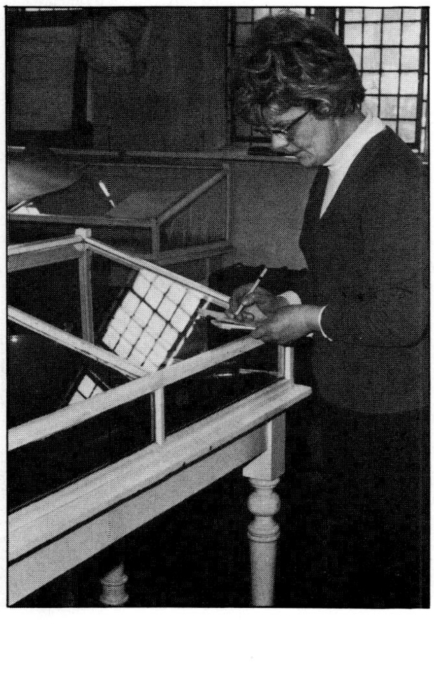

22. Selling sheep at Barnsley Cattle Market, Spring Bank Holiday 1985. Here a zoom lens has been used to isolate a group at a distance. It also tends to compress perspective, making the canteen in the background appear closer.

General Indoor Photography

Have you ever wondered why people on old indoor photographs appear so solemn and lifeless? The reason is that most pictures in less than ideal lighting conditions were taken with a long time-exposure, and a solemn expression is easier to hold. With modern equipment we are no longer handicapped by such problems and can capture smiles, fleeting expressions and party games. These latter are poorly represented in the historical record, with the exception of some royal charades and a few other very proper entertainments. It is in **your** hands to remedy this situation. Take your camera to parties, dinner meetings, etc. Try to bounce your flash off the ceiling for more even lighting, but don't bother too much if you cannot. Most people are flattered to be photographed, but be very careful f you catch them in undignified moments. It is usually safer to confine photography at parties to members of your own immediate circle. Naturally, if you ever consider publishing your pictures (even presenting copies to a museum constitutes publication) ask

23. Market day, July 1984. This picture concentrates on the people, always a good point. Surprisingly, though taken in the middle of the coal strike, very few men are visible. Is this coincidence, or the antipathy of the northern male to shopping?

permission from your subjects first. Above all, never assume that a couple who both wear wedding rings are married to each other, unless you know them personally. Distress, embarrassment, and even legal action can follow careless photography in social situations.

In this branch of our work captions are of vital importance. All relevant dates, names, locations etc. should be on the backs of prints. Use a proper pen and do **not** stick labels on with adhesive tape. To write on the back, lie the print on a sheet of glass or smooth formica to avoid embossing the front. If you keep your pictures or negatives make provision for them in the event of your death. Far too many photographs are burned when houses are cleared.

CHAPTER FIVE

Copying documents and images

Of all the detritus which humankind leaves in its wake, paper is amongst the most interesting. On it are the details of our lives, and those of our ancestors, set down in print and handwriting. Often it carries our vital images too, in the form of photographs, engravings and watercolours. This chapter will discuss how to copy most forms of documents and pictures. It will show how to eliminate stains, emphasise detail, and even help to make the invisible visible.

Copying is one of the most interesting and yet most involved tasks for the local history photographer. It has a mystique about it which makes it appear difficult and even slightly magical. In fact it is no more difficult than any other branch of photography once the principles are understood.

Having the right equipment for the job eases the task and, in fact, makes it quite enjoyable. Obviously documents and pictures do not come in one standard size, so different equipment is required according to the degree of magnification or reduction needed. Unfortunately for owners of compact cameras, this is one field where the SLR reigns supreme. Copying **is** possible with a compact, but is so complex that it is not worth the effort and the wasted film which inevitably results. This is because the compact has a separate viewfinder in the form of a window, usually above, and perhaps to one side, of the lens. This results in the viewfinder seeing a different image to the lens, a phenomenon called *parallax*. At normal distances this parallax is not at all important, but at close distances it makes the camera extremely difficult to use with any acccuracy.

For copying, then, our basic tool is the SLR. For originals over about A5 size, a *macro-zoom* lens will cope quite well, whilst full size plans and maps need no extra equipment. As the size of the original decreases, however, more specialised accessories become necessary. The cheapest close-up tool is a simple lens, the *close-up lens*, which is mounted in front of the lens in a simple holder. These are only about £3 each and come in a range of strengths, called *dioptres*. Number three is the one most generally useful, being the ideal size for copying postcards.

More expensive are *extension tubes*. These are precision machined tubes which hold the standard lens at a fixed distance from the film, thus achieving magnification without an extra layer of glass being involved. Though in theory tubes give better quality, in practice the difference is so small as to be negligible when the close-up lens is used with care. Tubes usually come in sets of three which can be used individually, or in any combination. Currently, a set of tubes costs about £35.

Finally, there are *bellows*. Bellows utilize the same principle as tubes but are continuously variable. Prices vary enormously from about £35 upwards, depending on the degree of automation provided between the camera body and the lens.

If the foregoing seems complex and expensive do not despair. Most local history work can be managed with a set of close-up lenses in combination with a standard lens. Even a good macro-zoom will do an adequate job. It all depends for what use the final picture is intended. If they are going to be published as large size colour illustrations in a coffee-table type book, then the purchase of a proper *macro lens* is advised. This will cost something over £100. Likewise, if massive display enlargements are envisaged. For all other purposes the close-up lens will suffice.

Whatever accessory is used the camera **must** be held rigid. All the main camera manufacturers produce a special *copy-stand*, but this is not really necessary. For over twenty years I have used an ordinary

25. A postcard copied with a three dioptre close-up lens. The contrast of the original lighting tends to block up the shadows. This is corrected by printing onto a softer grade of paper.

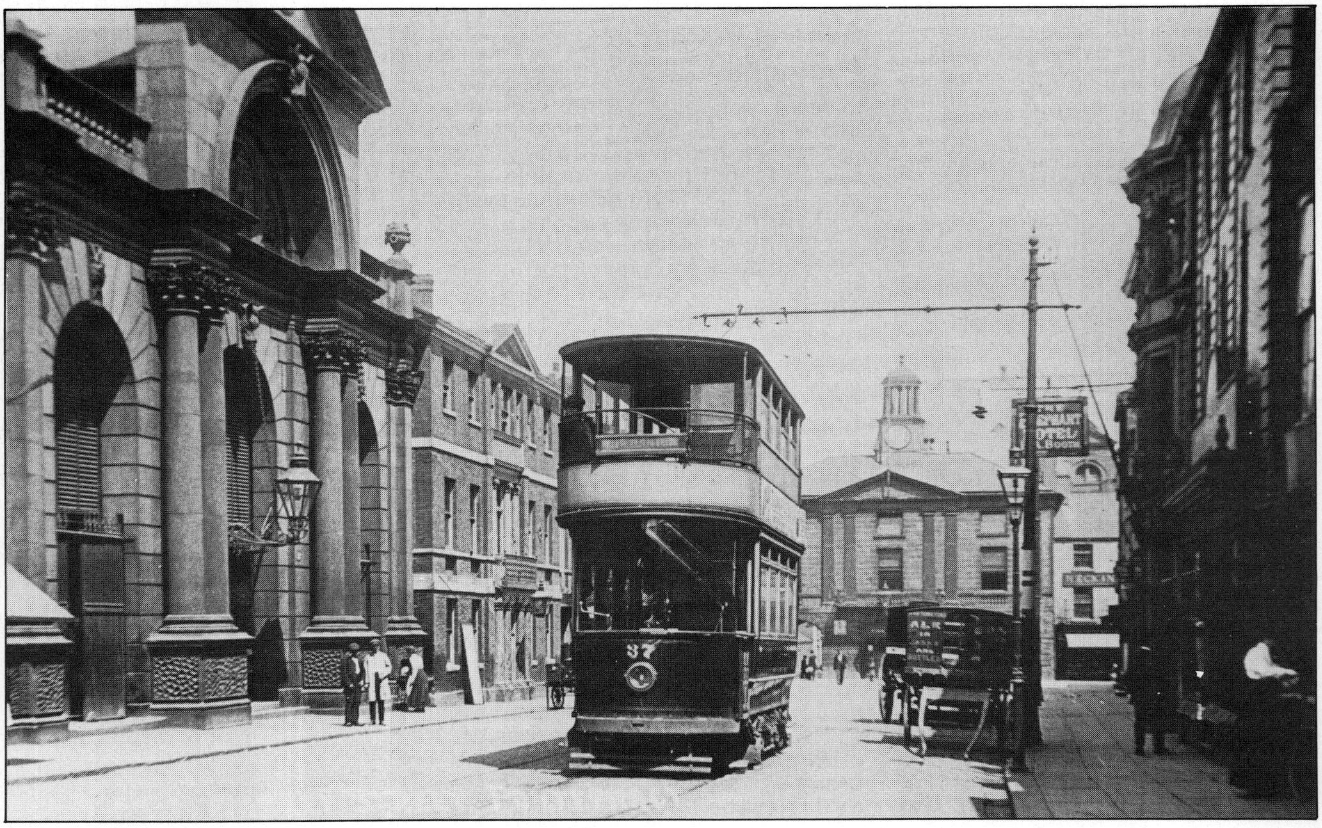

tripod with a ball and socket head mounted on the bottom of the centre-column. This is cheap, rigid, and adjustable. Some degree of DIY skill is unfortunately necessary, as the 1/4in Whitworth threaded screw must be fixed into the base of the ball and socket head. The real enthusiast will, of course, make his or her own, with taps and dies; the mechanically inept (like the writer) substitutes copious amounts of Araldite for skill, cutting a section of threaded steel from a bolt with a hacksaw!

A small spirit-level is needed to ensure that the back of the camera is truly level, and a *cable release* is essential to prevent vibration during the necessary long exposure. This latter is a mechanical or electrical switch on the end of a cable which is used flexed, so that the movement of tripping the shutter is not transferred to the camera body.

Copying of documents cannot be done efficiently without a set of *filters*. These are sheets of coloured glass or resin which go in front of the lens to emphasise or eliminate different colours in black and white. The most useful for our purpose are yellow, red, blue and sepia. Filters come in two basic types. Most useful in my opinion are system filters made by firms like Cokin, Ambico and Hoyarex. These are square or rectangular, fit standard holders, and can be adapted to any size of lens at little cost. Round filters are usually much more expensive and are individual to the front diameter of a single lens.

Lighting is important, but rather than spend a lot on special lights, trust in daylight helped by reflectors of white paper or even crumpled cooking foil.

The film you use will depend on the eventual use to which your pictures are put. I prefer to copy in monochrome, except for coloured originals, which tend to be rare in my preferred periods. Monochrome is cheaper, more flexible, allows the use of filters, and is permanent. If a slide is required, the monochrome picture can easily be re-photographed on colour film. Always choose a slow or medium speed monochrome film, like Ilford Pan F or FP4.

An unfortunate aspect of copying is that built-in exposure meters are nearly always wrong! Such meters are calibrated for average subjects, which usually means outdoor scenes. Professional photographers and really keen (and rich!) amateurs use a special *incident light meter*, which is an instrument which is placed on the copy-board and pointed at the camera lens to measure the light falling on the subject, rather than that reflected from it, as usual. Incident light meters are not cheap, at present starting at around £100. Again, there is a cheaper way out of this situation!

Ensure firstly, that the camera is set to manual exposure. If your camera is an auto-only instrument, you must use the *AE Lock* to lock in the reading obtained as below. Place a sheet of ordinary brown wrapping paper over your subject and take a meter reading from this. Experience has shown that this material perfectly simulates the 18% grey tone against which incident light meters are calibrated. Of course, a special 18% grey card can be purchased from your Kodak dealer if you feel that using bits of brown paper is beneath your dignity!

Types of subject

Engravings tend to be black or brown on a yellowed white background. This background generally records as a tone rather than white, as desired. This is where the filters come in. The rule to remember is that **a filter will lighten its own colour, and darken the opposite colour**. A light yellow filter should appreciably lighten the background of an old engraving, though if the ink is brown it may lighten this also. If this is likely to happen, use a yellow/green filter, or if you do not have one, place the green and the yellow together. The same principle works with accidental stains. The ubiquitous tea/coffee stain disappears magically when a sepia filter is used, whilst the common rust stains also disappear when a red or orange filter is tried. Needless to say, such magic is only possible with monochrome film. In addition, it must be remembered that each filter has a *factor*, an amount by which exposure must be multiplied in order to compensate for the light lost. This must be calculated extremely carefully, as any overexposure will eliminate the effect of the filter completely. This is another case where some bracketing is wise.

Old Photographs can vary from good, clear snaps to extremely faded and fragile specimens. **Never** attempt any form of cleaning on the original without the written permission of the owner. Curled and creased examples can be flattened under a sheet of glass, and external dirt can be moved with very careful application of *Teepol* on a barely damp cotton bud. Faded sepia images respond well to a blue filter. Once a good copy has been made much after-treatment, which would be dangerous on the original, is possible on the copy.

Enlarge the copy to about 8in by 10in on a matte or pearl surface. Any dark marks which filtration did not remove, like creases, *airbells*, etc.

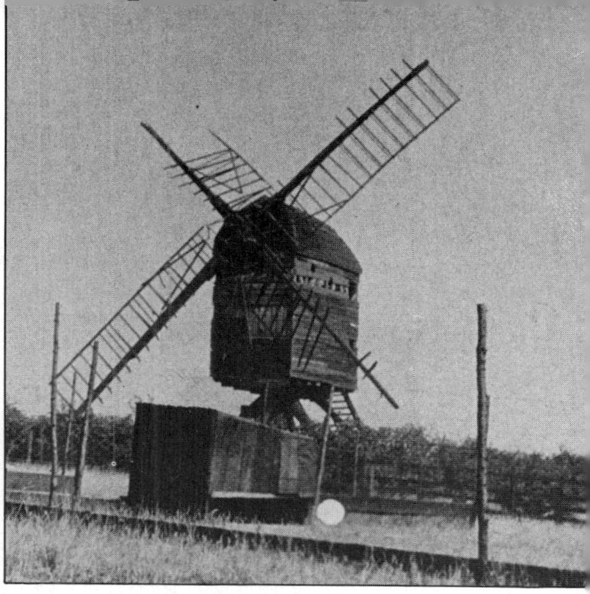

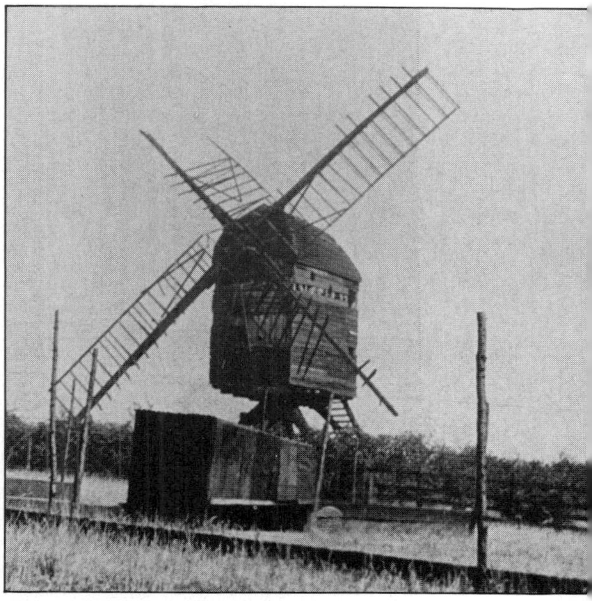

26. The tiniest original can often yield useful data. This windmill was photographed in the mid-nineteen thirties and my copy is from the middle of a one and a quarter inch contact print made then. The circular blemish is probably the result of an airbell in the printing. Note how dye-spotting makes it less apparent. Original picture by C Baines.

can be carefully bleached out using an 00 brush and ordinary medical iodine. Do not worry about the yellow stain left by the iodine; this is easily removed using the same 00 brush and ordinary photographic fixer of the non-hardening variety. Next, wash the print in running water to remove residual chemicals which, if left in, would cause their own staining after a year or two. Carefully squeegee the surface and dry the print on clean blotting paper. Light faults can now be carefully dotted in with a good photographic dye (about £2.50) used very dilute, and almost dry. Aim to simulate the grain pattern of the film itself, building up the density with successive applications of the dye. When the working copy is satisfactory, re-photograph it, over-exposing it by one stop and reducing development by about ten per cent, to keep contrast down. Needless to say,

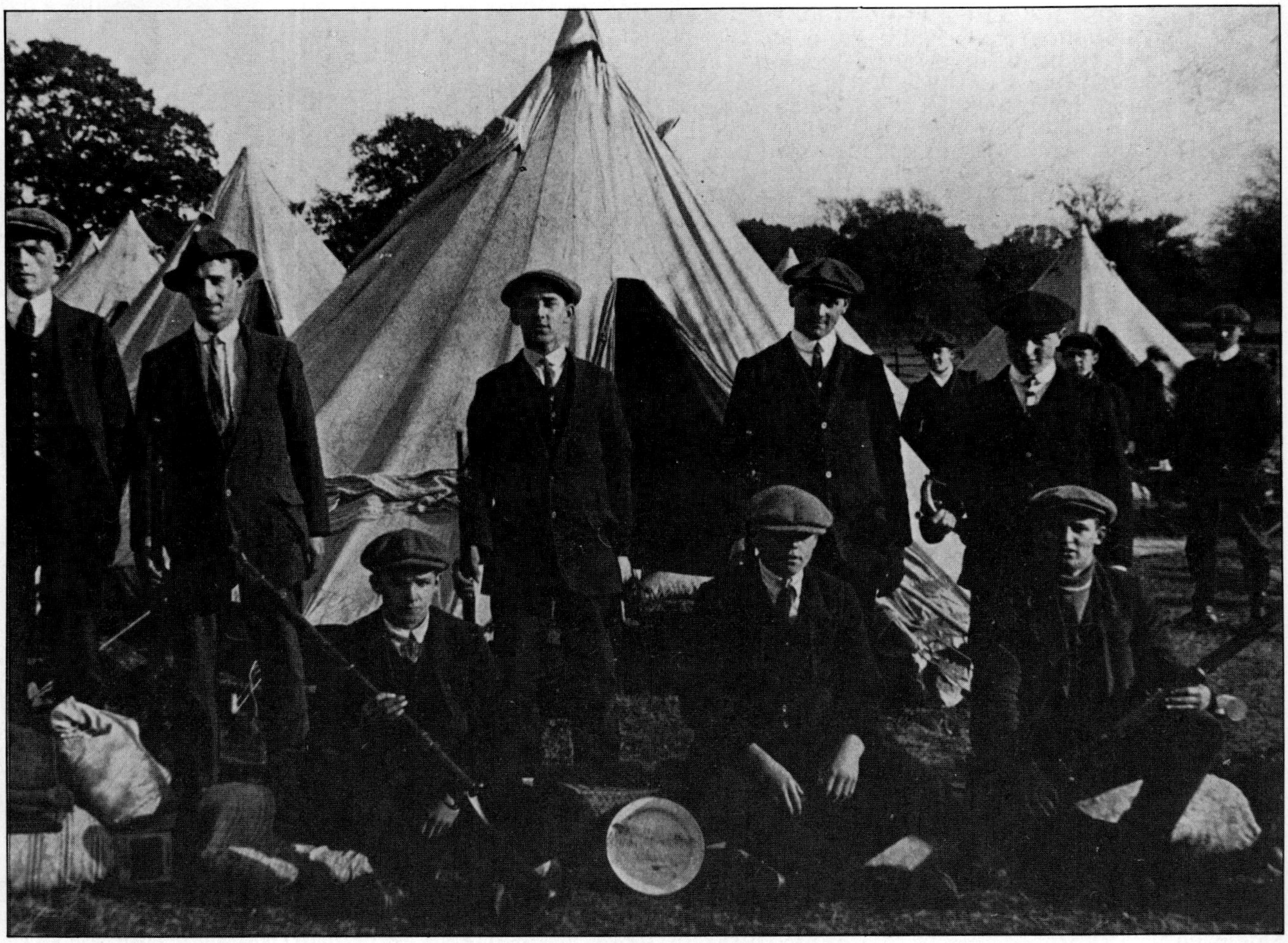

27. Surprising quality is possible from the tattiest originals. How many of these lads, I wonder, survived the Great War? Again, the copy was with a cheap close-up lens.

although these factors will give a workable negative, personal experiments may produce a better combination with your equipment. This final negative can now be used to make good quality prints which should be sepia-toned, not just to simulate age, but because toning vastly improves the keeping qualities of the image.

Paintings , if important, should be copied onto monochrome for the record. Colour is often more useful however, so a copy on a good, slow slide film ought to be made and printed on *Cibachrome*. Surface reflections are always a problem with oil-paintings, and you may have to experiment with matched oblique lighting from each side, or even with sheets of *polarizing* material, but here we enter the province of the specialised museum photographer, rather than the keen amateur. If reflections are still a problem after trying both these possibilities, then you may well be advised to pass the problem on to a professional who handles such subjects every day.

Lantern slides can be objects of beauty as well as repositories of historical data. They are well worth copying. Unfortunately projection slides tend to have too much contrast for a paper print so a soft film, in either monochrome or colour, is necessary. For black and white choose something moderately fast like HP5 at 400 ISO. A similar speed in colour film is about right, and I would choose Ektachrome 400 or 3M 400. Clean the slide thoroughly front and back, giving a final wipe with an anti-static cloth. Using Blu-tak fix a piece of drawing film to the back of the slide and then tape the whole assembly to a well-lit but shaded window. Surround the slide with dark paper to prevent unwanted light entering the camera lens and causing flare, then place the tripod-mounted camera in place, having first fixed on tubes or bellows. Focus carefully, stop down the lens to about f8, and expose, using the auto exposure mode or the manual mode. If large numbers of slides need copying it would probably be worth while to build a special duplicator.

Thirty five millimetre slides have now been in existence since the thirties, and good early examples of local subjects are well-worth copying. The technique outlined above is not precise enough for these small originals and a precision copier is a must. Currently a good one costs in the region of £30-£40. One very interesting early 35mm colour process is **Dufaycolour,** which utilised a very different principle to Kodachrome and Agfacolour, the two main types of colour film still in production. In many ways Dufaycolour was the forerunner of colour television and depends on a reseau of coloured particles. Extant examples still have beautiful colours, but are very dense compared to conventional slides. Luckily, the TTL metering system in a modern camera can deal very well with Dufaycolour, but the excessive contrast will often defeat the ordinary colour film. There are two possible solutions. The easiest is to copy on a soft colour negative film and then to have transparencies made from the negatives by a professional photofinishing service. This will not be cheap. The other way is to purchase proper slide duplicating film, made by both Kodak and Fuji, and copy onto this. Though seemingly easy, this is not, as duplicating film has no fixed speed value and trials must be made before a reliable procedure can be worked out. Even colour balance is not fixed, so trials must be made with *CC (Colour Correction)* filters as well.

Daguerreotypes, Tintypes, Ambrotypes etc. These early originals on metal or glass are really beyond the scope of the amateur, to whom this book is addressed. Being themselves highly reflective, attempts at photography often produce only an excellent image of the copy camera and its operator! If an attempt must be made, try surrounding the camera, tripod etc., but not the lens, in black velvet. Darken the room and light the subject very obliquely.

Handwritten Documents - Invisible Ray Techniques Of all the possible subjects to be copied, faded handwriting is the most challenging. It varies from the faintest sepia to a deep purple, but of course it is the faint variety which causes problems. Firstly, try to determine what colour the ink actually is. Then decide on a filter to deepen this colour, testing it first by a visual examination of the document through the filter. If all attempts fail using conventional filtration there is one other possibility before recourse to invisible ray techniques, and this is to think in terms of lightening the matrix, the paper or parchment on which the document is written, by using a filter of the same colour.

If this strategy too fails, then we must turn to the use of invisible ray techniques. Of the two, *ultraviolet* and *infra-red*, the former is probably the easiest for the non-professional, as UV light sources are easily available; most disco operators having at least one UV emitting bulb, whilst the fluorescence is visible to the eye in darkness. A fast monochrome film like HP5 is advisable, together with an *ultraviolet filter*, which removes the actual UV light which may cause flare whilst having no effect on the fluorescence.

Work in a room which can be blacked out. Set up the camera on a tripod as for normal copying and with an ultraviolet filter fitted. Arrange your UV light source to give oblique lighting to the document, placing a foil reflector at the other side if only one UV bulb or tube is available. It is most unlikely that any kind of exposure meter will be of any help, so be prepared to waste film, exposing

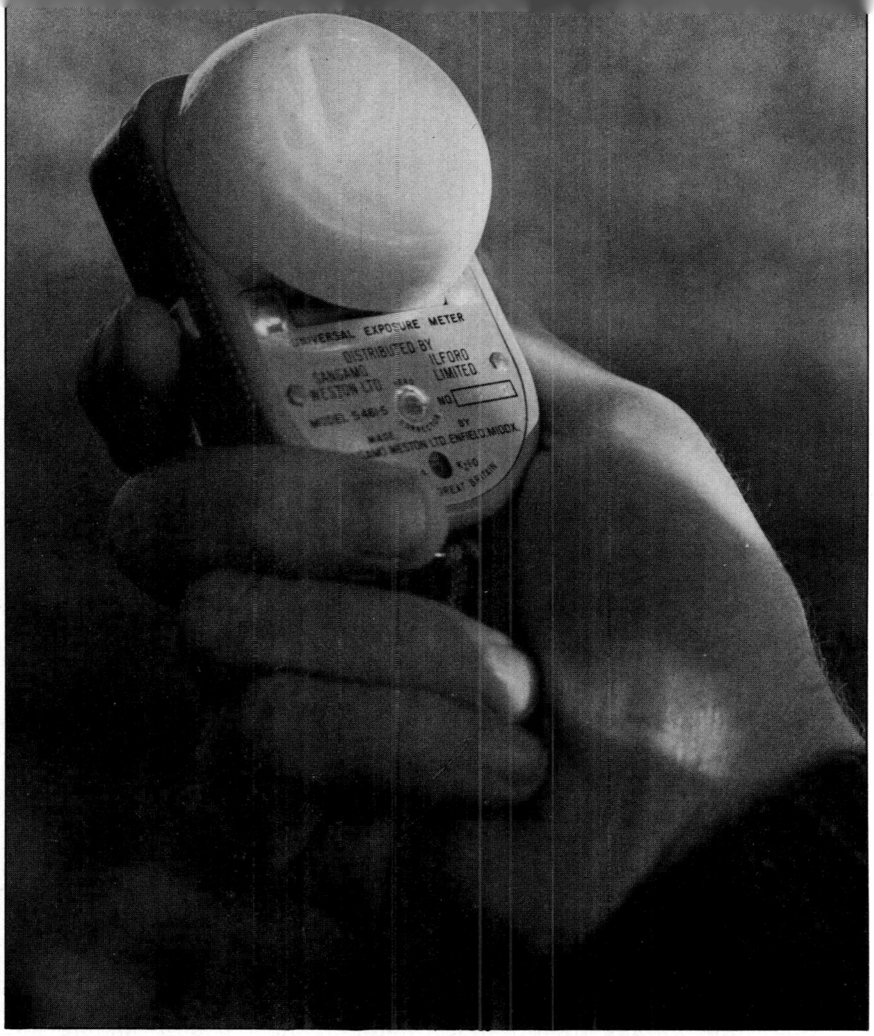

28. Using the incident light meter.

for five seconds initially, and steadily increasing by a factor of two each time. Develop normally, as recommended by the manufacturers of the film, and make a note of the frame which gives the best result. When in the future other UV pictures are needed, it is only necessary to duplicate lighting distances, exposure and development for perfect results.

One interesting point that I have not seen mentioned in any publications is that UV radiation causes headaches after constant use. It is considered to be harmless, but to avoid the headache, and any as yet unknown side effects, I try to avoid looking at the lamp, even wearing good quality sunglasses at times!

Infra-red is more difficult. Film is available from Kodak in both monochrome and colour. Follow the loading precautions mentioned in chapter three, and use a deep red filter for the mono film and a number 12 deep yellow filter for the colour version. For either, set a hand-held meter to 100 ISO and bracket exposures to ensure at least one good picture. The most reliable souce of IR radiation is ordinary electronic flash, and I have found, surprisingly, that an automatic flashgun set on auto gives excellent exposure for the colour infra-red film; I have yet to try the mono film with this light source. Processing for the mono version is quite easy as long as the special precautions are taken, but the colour IR Ektachrome demands *Process E4*, a process that few laboratories now use.

These invisible ray techniques are really for the committed photographer who does know his processing. Having said this, results can be spectacular and very worth while, but be prepared to expend both film and money!

CHAPTER SIX

Close-ups

The local historian requires photographs of all sorts of small objects, whether *in situ* or in the studio. The close-up is an art in itself, but it is one well worth mastering, as close-up pictures have an enormous impact, especially when shown on the projection screen as part of the illustration of a talk. In this chapter a few simple and effective techniques will be described which should meet all the historian's requirements.

Basic equipment for close-ups was described in the last chapter. One important piece of equipment not mentioned there is the *scale*. The viewer, on studying a picture, searches around it for visual clues to the dimensions of the objects illustrated. For this reason, all pictures of historical artifacts should contain a scale. The normal five or ten centimetre scale can be made at home from white card, using stencils or Letraset for any wording, as nothing looks as amateurish (in the worst sense of the word) as a hand-lettered scale. For larger objects, a human figure makes a good scale, as long as the person is not staring into the camera. Objects like gravestones, unless of unusual dimensions, do not really need a scale, though the modern trend towards increased precision could soon change this. For example, in one of his books the late Sir Mortimer Wheeler stated that an adult human skeleton does not need a scale in a normal record photograph, and he reiterated this advice to a friend in 1974. Yet today, little more than a dozen years later, when palaeopathologists are extracting more and more information from skeletons, at least one scale is vital with a skeleton.

My own advice is to err on the side of over-scaling, or to take the easy way out and take two pictures of any subject where scaling is of doubtful value, one with, and one without the scale! Therefore, a collection of scales of various sizes is important to the local history photographer, and again I would suggest a minimum collection of five, ten, and one hundred centimetre scales, preferably painted in black and white with the actual length stencilled neatly on each side.

The smaller ones can be made in a label-making machine, out of a material similar to Formica. These are extremely durable, my own having been in constant use for over a dozen years with few signs of wear. Larger ones of a metre or more are best made from strong timber which has previously been sanded and primed. Using really good quality white gloss paint, carefully paint the whole scale, giving at least two coats and allowing them to dry thoroughly between coats. Now, using a carpenter's square, carefully mark off the centimetre lengths and, using masking tape (purchased from a car accessory shop), isolate alternate sections. Paint the alternate sections with black gloss paint, again giving at least two coats, and peel off the masking tape whilst the black paint is dry but not hard. Finally, stencil 1 METRE on one of the smoother white sections near one end. The best stencils for this are the cheap ones obtained from the chain stationers in any High Street, whilst the best pens are spirit-based felt tips obtained from the same source.

When using a scale it is important that it be placed as close as possible to the object being recorded. Because of the foreshortening inherent in photographs, a scale wrongly placed will give a false impression of precision. Even the most respectable text books have made this mistake in the past.

Some subjects

Medium sized objects like gravestones and milestones must be photographed *in situ.* Mid to late afternoon in summer provides the ideal cross-lighting for gravestones which, of course, are all aligned the same way throughout Christendom. With milestones and wayside crosses, several visits may have to be made to discover the best lighting angle and it is worth being persistent in this. Though a piece of chalk can be useful to emphasise worn lettering, oblique lighting is better still. If, after all efforts to arrive at the best time, natural light cannot be used, then flash must be resorted to. There are two ways to approach this; the most companiable is to take a friend, but most friends baulk at the idea of spending an hour or so in the presence of a mute carving, so you may have to take two tripods and do it all yourself.

A powerful torch is useful as it can be used to find the best angle for the main flash, which of course will be placed well to one side. Having decided on this angle, place the flash either on a tripod or in the hands of your friend at this point, and set up the camera on another tripod, square on to the subject. Exposure must now be estimated, allowing for the natural light illuminating the face of the stone, **and** for the main flash off to one side. As an added complication, a smaller flash on the camera often helps the effect of relief that we are seeking to record. Those readers with one of the new generation cameras which can work all this out for them are at a great advantage here. The rest of us have to get involved in maths. Firstly, take an exposure meter reading of the main subject **remembering to do this at the flash synchronisation shutter speed.** Now find an auto setting of the main flash which will allow the **same** aperture. Stop down the camera lens one stop from this aperture, ie if it is f8, change it to f11. Set the smaller flash on the camera to its lowest power setting which should just add a little front lighting without affecting the exposure. The final result is our basic exposure which should give a usable result in monochrome and colour negative. With slide film, some *bracketing* is advised. There are two ways of synchronising the flashes in this set-up. The cheapest is to use a flash extension cable and a double flash connector, but the most efficient is to fit a *slave* to the main flash and let the impulse from the smaller gun on the camera fire it.

Well-worn low relief objects need a particular form of oblique lighting from multiple flashes. This technique was developed by Geoff Quick ARPS of the Royal Commission for Historic Monuments (Scotland) to record the West Highland Stones, a series of extremely worn gravestones in churchyards situated along the northwest coast of Scotland. The method involves the simultaneous firing of four flashes at an extremely acute angle across the face of the stone, one from each side. *Ambient* light must be completely eliminated, so the photography is best done at night, and can cause problems with passers by, who sometimes get the wrong idea on seeing flashes and dim figures moving around burial grounds at night! It is a somewhat complex technique but the results are always worth the considerable effort.

Stained glass, in contrast, is an easy subject to record. The greatest problem for the amateur is that of getting the camera to the correct height, as any tilting will distort the result. A sunny day is to be avoided, the best lighting coming from a bright but overcast sky. When these conditions are combined with snow the lighting for most stained glass windows is perfect. Some effort must be made to lift the camera and tripod to the height of the centre of the window. Having done this, fit the longest focal length lens that will

29. Wall-mounted memorial from St Michael's parish church, Carleton. Lighting was one powerful flashgun held to the left of the memorial and aimed to 'graze' the surface. The camera was on a tripod, with a 35-70mm zoom lens at about 40mm. The flash was on a long extension, held by the photographer, the exposure being made with the self-timer. The cluttered surroundings detract from the impact of the memorial, so its image was cut from the print and mounted onto black glossy board.

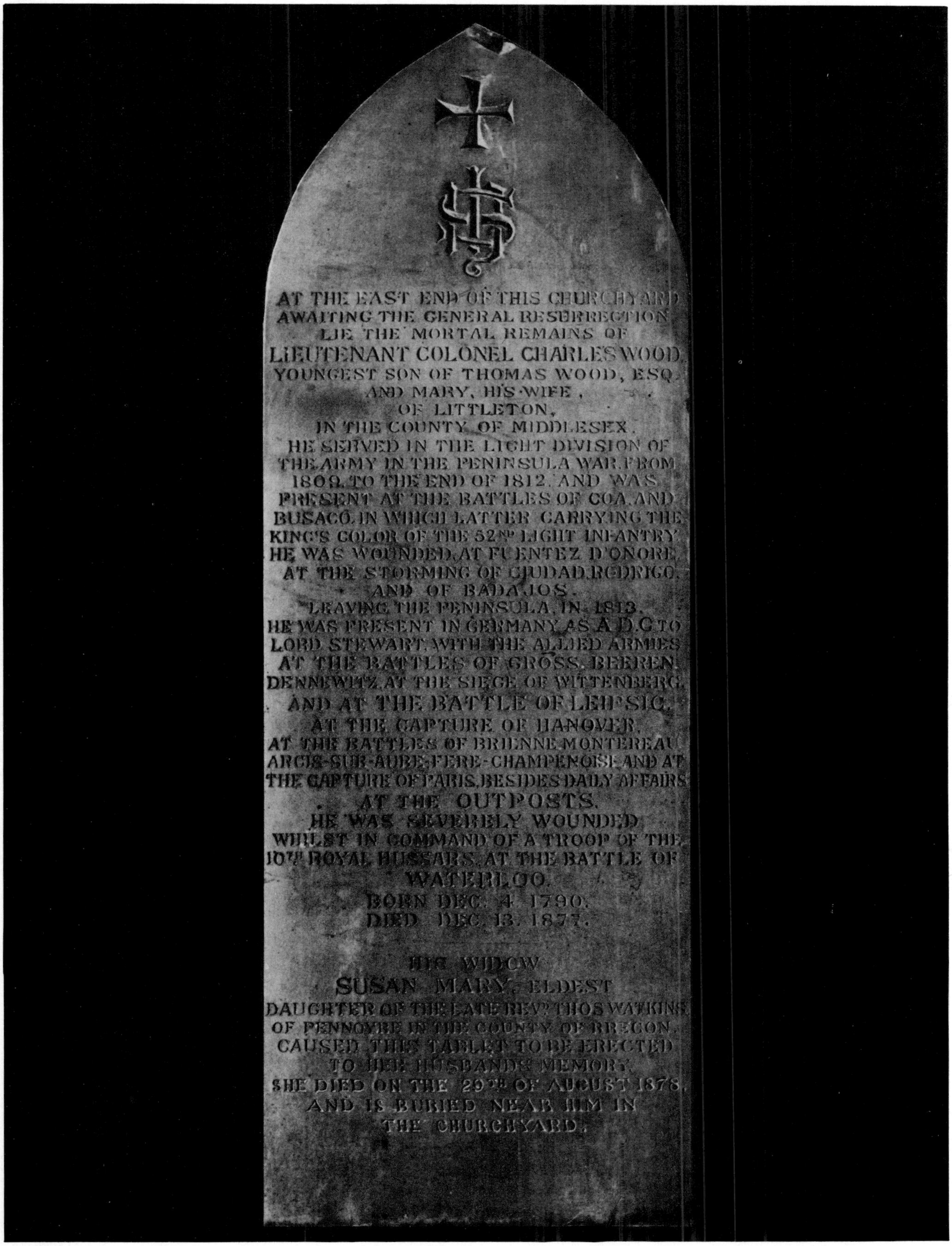
AT THE EAST END OF THIS CHURCHYARD
AWAITING THE GENERAL RESURRECTION
LIE THE MORTAL REMAINS OF
LIEUTENANT COLONEL CHARLES WOOD.
YOUNGEST SON OF THOMAS WOOD, ESQ.
AND MARY, HIS WIFE,
OF LITTLETON,
IN THE COUNTY OF MIDDLESEX.
HE SERVED IN THE LIGHT DIVISION OF
THE ARMY IN THE PENINSULA WAR FROM
1809, TO THE END OF 1812, AND WAS
PRESENT AT THE BATTLES OF COA, AND
BUSACO, IN WHICH LATTER CARRYING THE
KING'S COLOR OF THE 52ND LIGHT INFANTRY
HE WAS WOUNDED, AT FUENTEZ D'ONORE,
AT THE STORMING OF CIUDAD RODRIGO,
AND OF BADAJOS.
LEAVING THE PENINSULA, IN 1813,
HE WAS PRESENT IN GERMANY AS A.D.C TO
LORD STEWART, WITH THE ALLIED ARMIES
AT THE BATTLES OF GROSS, BEEREN,
DENNEWITZ, AT THE SIEGE OF WITTENBERG,
AND AT THE BATTLE OF LEIPSIC,
AT THE CAPTURE OF HANOVER,
AT THE BATTLES OF BRIENNE, MONTEREAU,
ARCIS-SUR-AUBE, FERE-CHAMPENOISE AND AT
THE CAPTURE OF PARIS, BESIDES DAILY AFFAIRS
AT THE OUTPOSTS.
HE WAS SEVERELY WOUNDED
WHILST IN COMMAND OF A TROOP OF THE
10TH ROYAL HUSSARS, AT THE BATTLE OF
WATERLOO.
BORN DEC. 4. 1790.
DIED DEC. 13. 1877.
HIS WIDOW
SUSAN MARY, ELDEST
DAUGHTER OF THE LATE REVD THOS WATKINS
OF PENNOYRE IN THE COUNTY OF BRECON,
CAUSED THIS TABLET TO BE ERECTED
TO HER HUSBAND'S MEMORY.
SHE DIED ON THE 29TH OF AUGUST 1878,
AND IS BURIED NEAR HIM IN
THE CHURCHYARD.

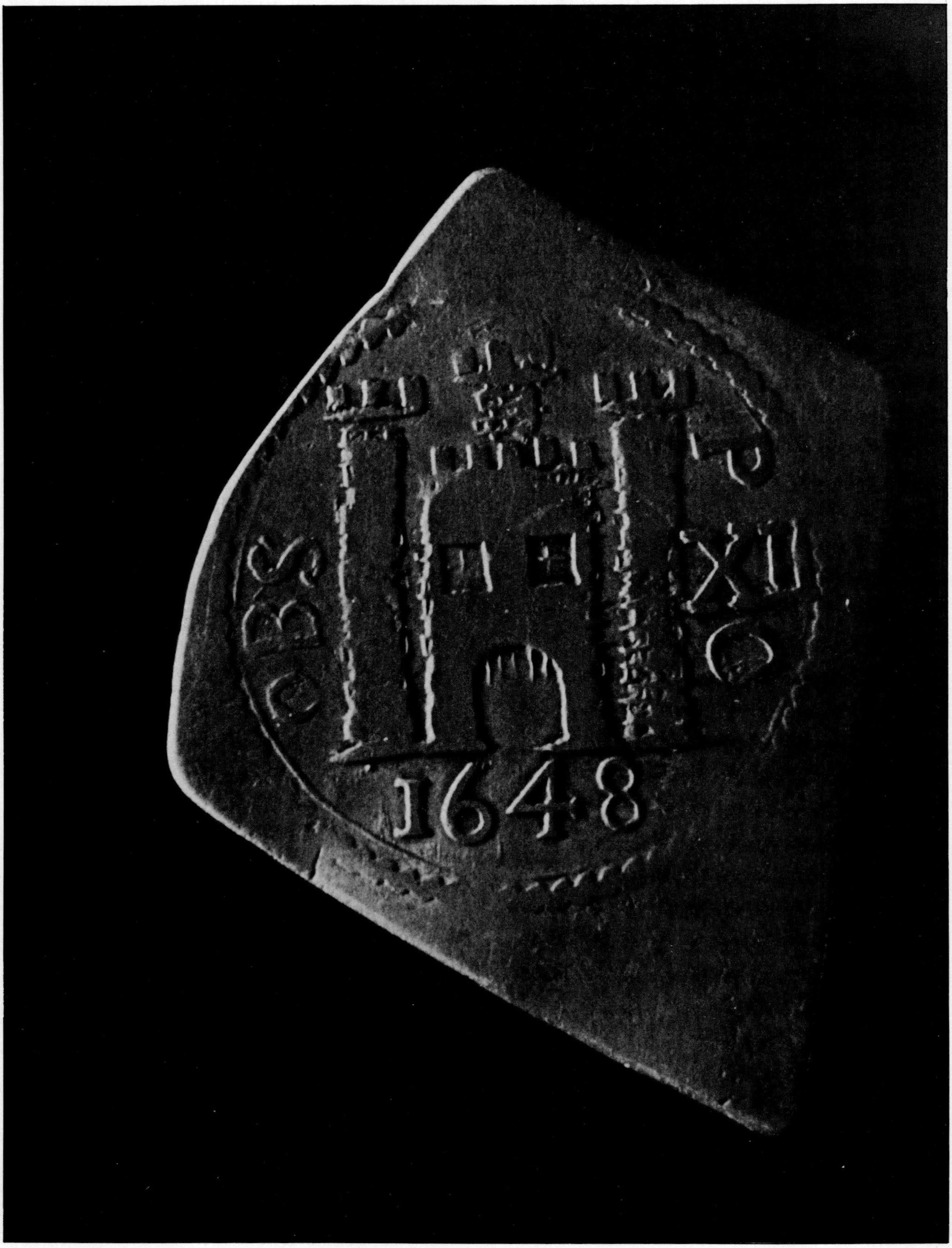
XII
1648

allow the subject to fill the frame. Stained glass, being a self-illuminating subject, nearly always responds to automatic exposure with both types of colour film, though some *bracketing* is advisable with monochrome. For all this, of course, it is assumed that the Vicar's permission has been sought well in advance.

Smaller objects can usually be transported to a convenient location for photography. Very few people in the historical field possess a proper studio, but a few sheets of pastel card, a piece of glass, and some other odds and ends will enable several basic set-ups to be constructed which, if used carefully, will help to produce pictures of studio quality. Though my diagrams show lamps in use, the beginner would be wiser using daylight to begin with, only graduating to proper photographic lighting with increasing experience. Membership of a photographic society is really useful in this area, as most clubs have lights, reflectors, proper background supports and even rolls of coloured background paper which can often be borrowed by members.

Of the three basic set-ups illustrated, the curved card is best for largish items like pots and statuettes. The raised glass technique is useful for small artefacts, whilst the darkbox gives a beautiful black background for coins. In all these it is useful to know that it is the convention for the main light to come from the top left of the subject and that scales should always be in the chief plane of the subject.

One interesting and unusual method not illustrated here makes use of a cheap white plastic lampshade of the kind usually found in bathrooms. It must be open top and bottom. The small object to be photographed is placed on a white card with the light fitting over it. Place the camera so that it looks straight down into the top, and use two small flashguns or daylight with reflectors to light the outside of the fitting. For larger objects requiring similar lighting, borrow the frame of a Wendy House, cover it in muslin, leaving a hole for the lens to peep through. Again, point plenty of light at it from several directions.

Most 'studio' work of this kind is easier than you think, as long as you get the set-up right, estimate the exposure well, *bracketing* where necessary, and carefully examine the viewfinder image to ensure that everything is perfect **before** exposure.

30. Civil War siege coin, Pontefract.

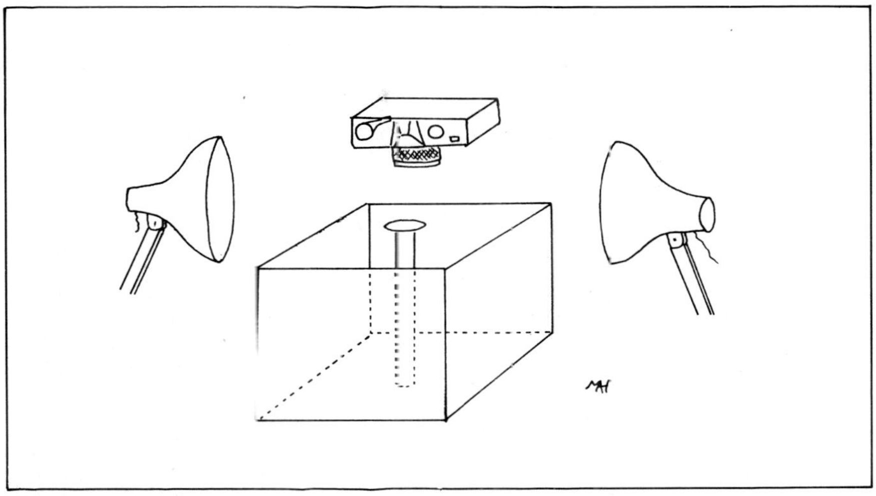

THE DARKBOX TECHNIQUE

An ordinary cardboard box is painted matte black inside. The subject is suspended level with the top of the box either on blackened dowel or on a piece of glass. Lighting is arranged so that the interior of the box is in total shadow.

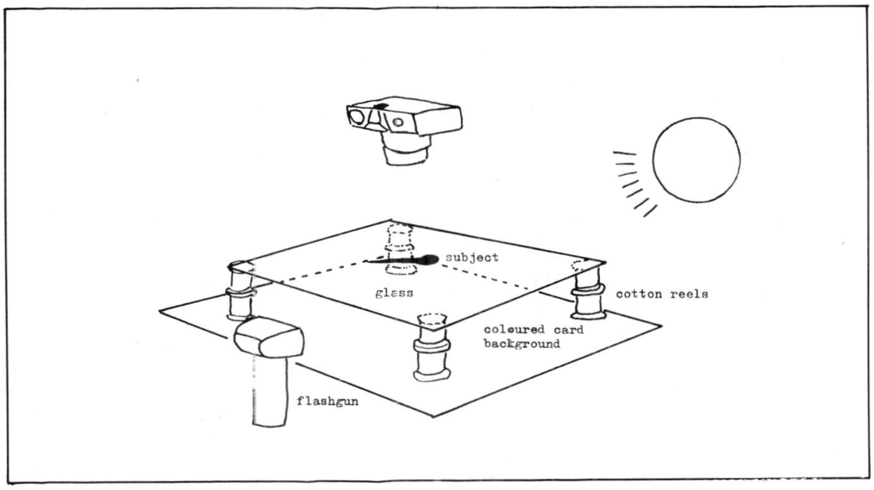

THE RAISED GLASS TECHNIQUE

This method is self-explanatory. The flash unit can be dispensed with if you ensure that no shadows are cast on the background. The camera must, of course, be supported.

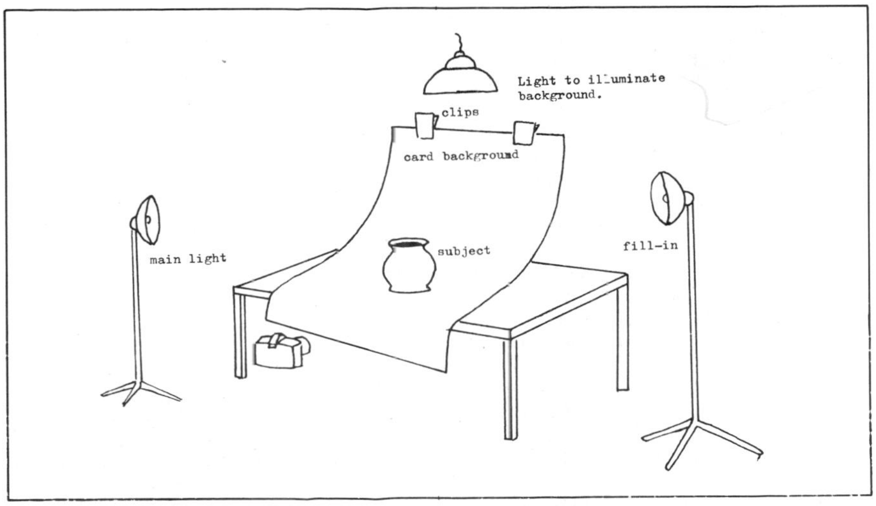

THE CURVED CARD TECHNIQUE

Before exposing, check through the viewfinder to make sure that the lighting is even to give correct modelling. There should be no shadows on the card behind the subject and only a faint one to its right.

CHAPTER SEVEN

Illustrating Books, Articles and Lectures

Apart from archive storage, photographs are chiefly of value as illustrations for books, articles and lectures. Unfortunately there still exists an attitude in some societies that any image produced by a camera is adequate for reproduction. Such people lump together trade enprints, slides and even negatives and expect a printer to produce perfect illustrations from the most imperfect materials. Others imagine that, as colour pictures in books are printed on paper, paper prints are necessary as the first step. Another misconception, in this case popular amongst photographers, is that monochrome prints for reproduction must be printed onto the most contrasty paper. Finally, in some quarters, there is the belief that high quality half-tone illustrations can be made direct from negatives.

Monochrome illustrations

For black and white pictures, the very best quality glossy prints are required, though Ilford Pearl comes a close second. They must have a full range of tones, be borderless (though the US print market prefers a quarter-inch white border) and be printed to A4 or 8in x 10in. This latter size is the current minimum used by professional and serious amateur photographers for most purposes, though more and more are changing to A4 as it most nearly matches 35mm negative format. Thus it has the advantage that just about everything seen in the viewfinder can be printed without either trimming the print or missing off the edges of the negative. For adequate reproduction prints must begin with good negatives and the only way to achieve these is to develop the film yourself. This is quite straightforward as long as the manufacturer's instructions are followed exactly in regard to time, temperature, dilution etc.

If the original is a colour transparency there are two ways of obtaining mono prints for reproduction. The first is costly and involves using a professional photofinishing house to make a negative from the slide and print from this. The second is cheaper and, because it involves one less stage, generally more effective, as long as the slide involved is not too contrasty. It is to have a glossy *Cibachrome* print made direct from the slide. Such prints have a unique high-gloss finish which reproduces well as a monochrome. Much depends, of course, on what type of reversal film was used for the original transparency, but in the examples which I have submitted for publication on past occasions, even the older, grainier films of twenty years ago have come out well.

If the original is on colour negative film then a good glossy print of the correct size must be made from the negative. In this case there is no advantage in having a colour print, except that it is usually cheaper to have a good colour print made commercially than a good monochrome one. If you do your own printing and have not yet tried to print mono from colour negatives, use a variable contrast paper like Ilford *Multigrade* and try the higher contrast filters from four upwards. These tend to compensate for the orange mask in the negative. Colour negatives really need a *panchromatic* printing paper which, as its name suggests, is sensitive to all colours. This means that no safelight can be used, and that processing must really be carried out in a colour drum. For just a few prints this is hardly worth the effort, which is why I recommend printing on variable contrast paper.

Colour illustration

Colour is not cheap, so only opt for it if transparencies of really good quality are available. Of course 'quality' is a relative term, but slides which show signs of colour-cast, unsharpness or fingerprints should be rejected out of hand. The bigger the slide, the better it will be to reproduce, so that a 4in x 5in or two and a quarter inch square slide will give much better reproduction than a 35mm. If 35mm is unavoidable then use a slow film like Fujichrome 50 ISO in good light with a tripod and a cable release.

Cleanliness if vital, and the slide should also be examined for scratches. Any on the *emulsion* side cannot be treated at all, but scratches on the *film base* can often be treated with a special laquer which has the same refractive index as the film. It is called *Lamitol* and is at present only available from one mail-order photographic supplier.

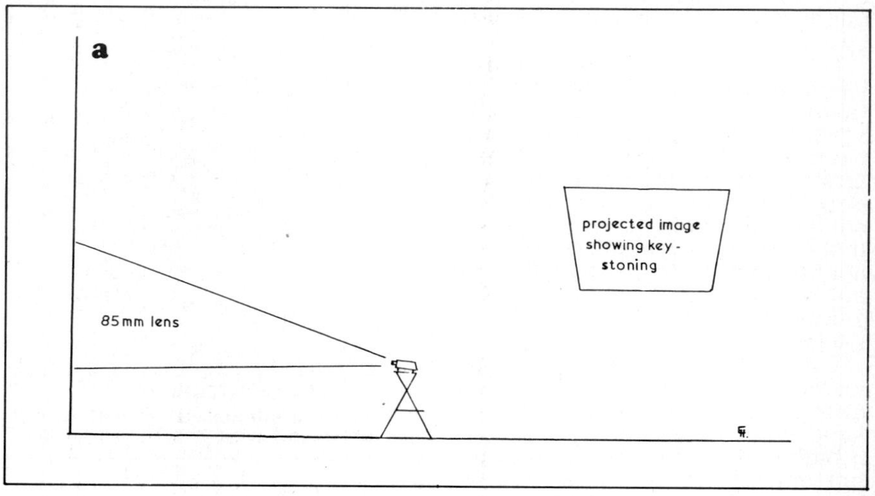

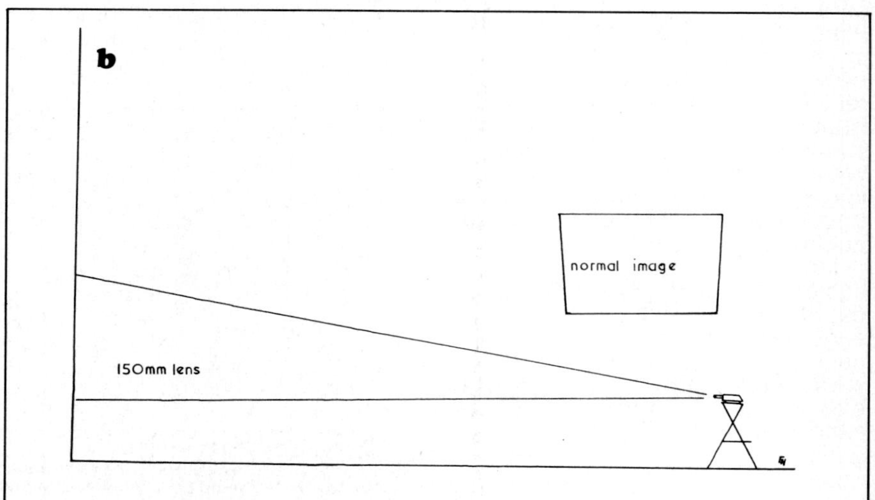

Captions

For prints, the caption, plus any acknowledgments, should be on the back. But **never** write on the back of a print destined for reproduction, as any embossing will show through. A far better way is to type captions onto adhesive paper and lightly stick this, by one end only, onto the reverse side. For picture credits (picture by...) I use the tiny self-adhesive labels which are advertised in all the Sunday papers. These go directly onto the back of the print, so that even if the caption comes off the origination of the print is still clear. For esoteric subjects an arrow and word 'top' help the layout artist to get the picture the right way up.

Colour-captions should be typed onto a separate sheet and keyed to the transparencies by numbers on the mounts. Use a proper pen rather than the tiny self-adhesive spots which always migrate to the emulsion surface. The photographer's name and address can go on the reverse of the mount or, in the case of larger sizes, on the transparent envelope in which the slide is kept. Always indicate which is the front of a slide and, again for unusual subjects, which way up it should appear.

Always try to acknowledge the photographer. You would be horrified if you wrote a book and the publishers refused to acknowledge you as author, but too many local historians do exactly the same thing to the photographer without even thinking.

It is a sobering thought that most books on local history are bought by people whom we would class as only mildly interested in the subject. Our problem is to persuade such people to buy our books, thus subsidising our interest and research. The best persuasion is a well laid-out book with plenty of good, relevant pictures. We live in a visual age and anyone who does not utilise its technology when it is freely and cheaply available is unlikely to succeed.

Basic Techniques for Illustrated Lectures

As an inveterate lecture-goer I see hundreds of talks at local history, archaeological and photographic societies. A frequent speaker myself, I often squirm with embarrassment for the sake of either guest speakers or societies. There appears to be a type of person who imagines that any projector will show anything from 16mm sound movies to the old three and a quarter inch slides. Unfortunately, this type of person is often to be found in a position of authority in local societies. Small wonder then that in some groups presentation of lectures leaves much to be desired. Then there is the speaker who believes that he/she is so good that he/she can hold an audience for one and a half hours without need of any visual assistance other than a dozen dirty fingerprinted Kodachromes projected onto an off-white wall. Imagine the effect of this on a prospective member.

One cannot give a decent lecture without some form of illustration. Although movie-film, videotape and *OHP transparencies* all have a role, the best form of lecture illustration to date is the colour transparency. Bigger slides give much better quality but the sheer versatility and convenience of the equipment in this size, both for taking and for projecting the image, make it unbeatable.

When preparing a set of slides for a lecture the following considerations should be borne in mind.

Consistency Though modern films are all excellent, they each have minor characteristics which only become evident in comparison. Therefore, it is wiser to stick to one make of film if at all possible. When this is not possible, try to match films with similar characteristics, eg both Fuji and Agfa films tend towards a warm rendering, so they usually mix better than, say, Kodak Ektachrome, which is cold, with Agfa. However, Konica film has a more neutral rendering so this goes quite well with either the warm or the cold film.

Plan Ahead You usually have an idea if a project you are working on will become the subject of a lecture. Always keep this in mind, and shoot plenty of slides at varying angles and focal lengths. Try to think in terms of film-making and vary between wide-views, medium shots and close-ups. Shoot plenty of continuity and people-at-work pictures.

Maps, Diagrams etc. Maps and diagrams from books are rarely suitable for lecture illustration. Text is too small and lines too thin to be seen from the back of a room. The answer is to re-draw maps and diagrams using thicker lines and larger, less cluttered text. Light lines on a dense background show even better in projection. Shoot at least three slides of each item; this is much better than reversing the projector when you need to refer to the same picture more than once during the talk.

Mounting Slides in *readymounts* are **not** ready for projection. These thin card or plastic frames are solely intended to assist in preliminary sorting and editing. Once you have selected your lecture-set, mount each slide in a proper plastic with glass frame. The best are *Gepe* (pronounced Geepee) and *Quickpoint*. The Gepe mounting press works equally well with either make of frame, but it is important to ensure that the slides are dry before mounting, and are kept in an atmosphere with a humidity level of less than 40%. Brown patches appearing during projection are the result of dampness, and can be eliminated by placing a sachet of *silica gel* with the slides a few days before they are needed. The silica gel must be re-generated in an oven before use, but this precaution is well worth the effort. Multi-coloured patterns on the slide during projection are called *Newton's Rings* and are the result of interference between the smooth film-base and the smooth glass. They can be prevented by using mounts with special anti-Newton Ring (AN) glass, which is etched to prevent perfect contact. When purchasing Gepe mounts you must specify AN glass, but Quickpoint mounts have it fitted as standard on the correct side of the mount.

Technical aspects of projection for societies and speakers.

Projectors. Using an antique one-at-a-time projector is an insult to a speaker, a danger to the slides, and a recipe for disaster. These old machines use a mains voltage lamp which, by modern standards, generates far too much heat. Every second a slide stays in the gate reduces its life considerably. Whilst the fact that each individual slide must be handled both before and after projection increases the risk of dropping, damage and fingermarking.

There are two common automatic projector types in general use at present. The Kodak *Carousels* take circular trays each holding eighty slides. The DIN standard projectors (made by many different manufacturers) take long trays holding thirty-six or fifty slides. These two types are **not** compatible and, confusingly, many of the DIN standard machines will also take other loading systems like the GAF Rototray, which is a circular upright drum not unlike a Carousel tray, or the Agfa CS system which depends upon a special very thin mount. Most universities and museums use Carousels, so speakers from such establishments will bring slides in Carousel trays. Amateurs, and many people in the lower echelons of

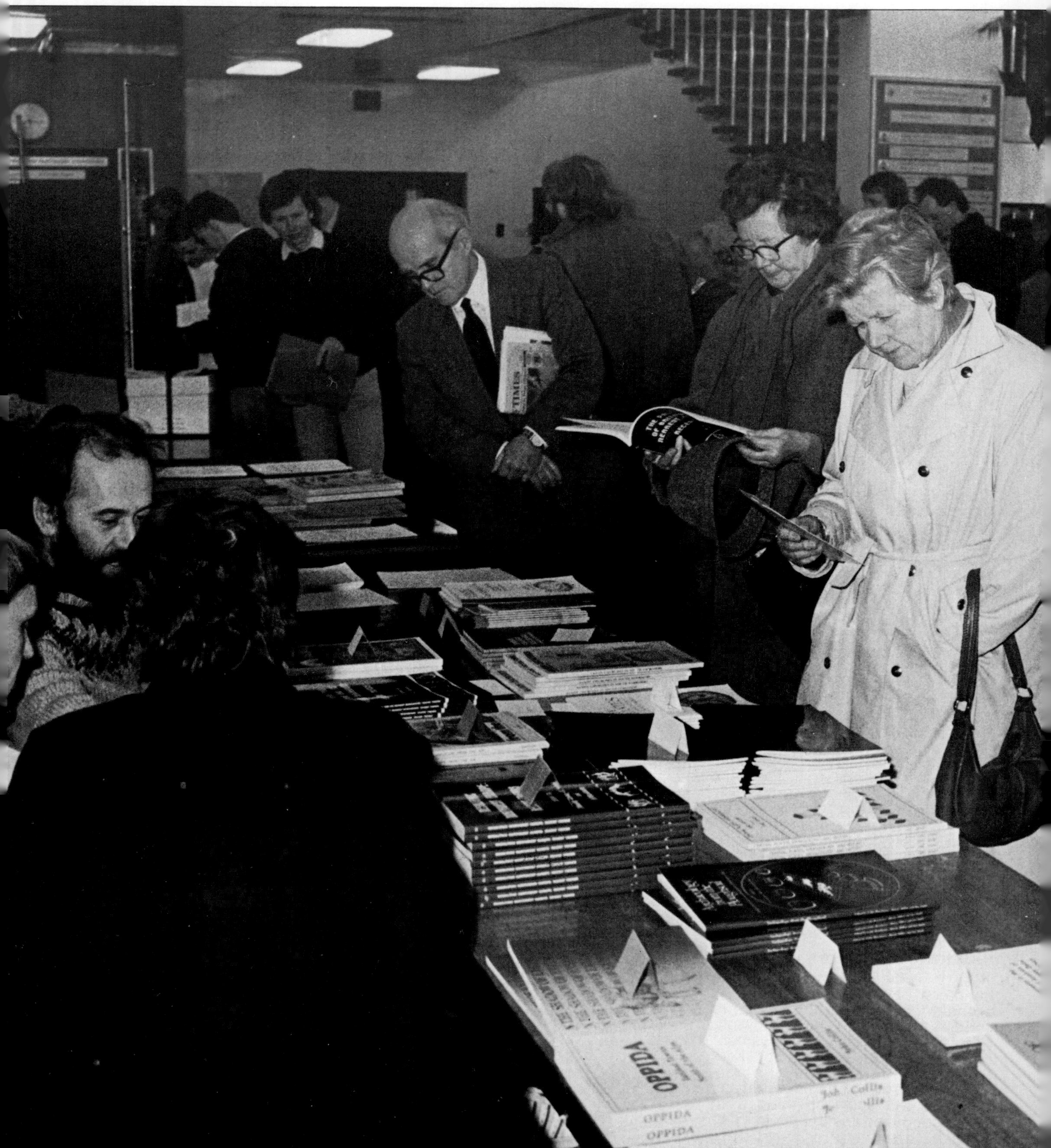
OPPIDA
OPPIDA
OPPIDA

education, use the DIN machines which are generally, but not invariably, cheaper. The answer for any society is to have a sufficient number of the right type of tray available so that slides can be changed before and after the talk. Carousel trays must be zeroed before use; to do this, first ensure that the transparent plastic dust-cover is firmly in position, to hold any slides in place, and then turn the tray upside down. Now, rotate the metal base in any direction until it stops with a click. Failure to do this makes transport of the slide impossible, as a local society found to their cost when they borrowed a Carousel and failed to read the instructions!

A lens of at least 100mm focal length is needed in order that the machine sits well back from the screen. Even better is the 150mm, which fills a five foot screen at twenty feet. The 80mm lens supplied as standard with many projectors today is designed to give a big picture in a small room. Apart from the fact that it is often an inferior plastic optic, its short throw is totally unsuitable for public performances.

Focussing Auto-focussing is wonderful for regular speakers who mount each slide properly. I find that it relieves me of having to watch the screen as each slide comes up, so that the commentary is more spontaneous. However, for societies providing facilities for different speakers, many of whom leave the slides in readymounts, it is a menace. It works by shining a small light onto the front of the slide at an angle. The size of the light spot is calculated by a sensor which is connected to a motor on the lens-mount, which pushes the lens in and out as necessary. With a slide in a readymount this produces a lot of 'tracking' as the film warms up and expands. Unfortunately, too, the sensor-spot may not be on the part of the slide that you want to be sharp. In the case of glass mounts the slide is kept perfectly flat so that it is all sharp, and all subsequent slides are sharp. Therefore, for a society, remote focus with a long extension lead is preferable. Any speaker who wishes to change and focus him/herself can do so; those who do not can leave it in the hands of a projectionist who, sitting in the audience near the machine, can do everything except change trays by remote control.

31. Pictures of meetings, conferences and symposia are rarely taken, but will prove to have increased value as time goes on.

Screens Slides can be vertical or horizontal, so that a square screen is needed. The best surface is matte white; this allows viewing at all angles. *Beaded screens* are not suitable for public showings other than in long, narrow rooms. A really good screen can be produced simply and cheaply by painting a suitable wall with brilliant white matte emulsion, but it must be protected in some way between use. Next best is a fixed roller screen. Its size will depend a lot on the size of the room, the power of the projector and the number of people who are expected at any one time. Most societies tend to make do with a small portable screen, when any modern projector in an efficient blackout will fill a six foot screen. A reasonable compromise would be a big wall prepared as described, or a ten foot roller screen. This enables a 250 watt machine like the Carousel to give a big image, or the more common 150 watt machine to produce a six foot image.

The Room Projectors only work in the **dark.** Any reading light must be well shielded from the screen and glass partitions into other room be well covered.

Preparation & Precautions The projector must be at 90 degrees to the screen and not tilted up too much, as shown in figure 1. This is why long focus lenses are necessary, as the further back the machine sits, the less tilt is necessary to achieve a high image. Needless to say any projector table must be firm with a hard top, both to ensure the stability of the image and to prevent the air intake being obstructed. If this eventuality does occur, a thermal cut-out will switch off the bulb. Resetting is sometimes necessary, and the switch for this is sited in different places on different machines. At least one spare bulb of the correct type and a few spare fuses should be kept with the projector, as well as a battery-powered light pointer.

Our work as photographers in local history reaches the enthusiast and the general public via publication and projection. By following the advice given above, a good impression should be made on everyone.

CHAPTER EIGHT

Aerial Photography

Aerial pictures have numerous uses in local history. More so even than a map, an air photograph shows at a glance the original layout of a settlement, its subsequent expansion or contraction, and the lines of communication, both ancient and modern. Though aerial photographs can be bought, those commonly available may not be at the right scale or may have been taken in poor lighting conditions. The remedy, as usual, is to take your own.

Aerial photography is a perfect subject for the modern automatic exposure camera, whether it be compact or SLR. Add an *auto winder* and perhaps a *data-imprinting back* and you have the ultimate recording instrument. Film type must be chosen with care in view of the high cost of each flight, but also bearing in mind the uses to which the pictures will be put. For myself, I always fly with at least two cameras, one loaded with FP4 and the other with Fujichrome RDP 100. If colour prints are subsequently needed then *Cibachrome* will give all the quality required. The camera with monochrome always carries an orange filter, whilst the one with colour always has at least an *ultra violet filter*and sometimes a *polarizing* filter. When buying filters, do not be persuaded into buying a haze filter instead of a proper UV. (Some shop assistants will try to sell you one of these if they do not have the real thing in stock, but the haze filter can add an unnatural pinky/brown cast to your slides). Both cameras carry a standard 50mm or 55mm lens and a metal *lens hood*. This latter accessory is more important than ever in the air, as it prevents extraneous light causing flare inside the camera. Rubber ones can distort in the slipstream & obscure part of the image.

If you are flying with a friend from the local aero club it is unlikely that you will be able to choose the type of aeroplane. Aerial work is possible from all machines, but certain types are better than others. In my experience, the very best types are the high wing monoplanes like the Piper Cub and the Cessna 150. In these it is possible to open a window or a door so that, with the plane in a bank, the photographer is in an ideal position to shoot with the wing shading the lens from direct sunlight. The Cessna 172 is also good, but as the observer's window does not usually open, the photographer must sit behind the pilot and shoot over his shoulder. This necessitates removing the safety harness! Incidently, for those with a fear of heights, there is no sensation of altitude when leaning out of an aircraft with a camera.

The low wing machines tend to have perspex hoods which cannot be opened in flight. Though photography is possible, the image is bound to suffer, as it must pass through the scratched perspex before entering the lens. This effect can be minimised by using a medium wide angle lens such as a 35mm focal length. The gliders I have flown in have suffered from the same problem, whilst my only two efforts from helicopters convinced me that a fixed wing machine is easier and more comfortable. I have yet to try photography from an open cockpit biplane or an airship, though I have been given to understand that the

32. View from the rear seat of a Cessna 172, looking over the pilot's shoulder through the open window.

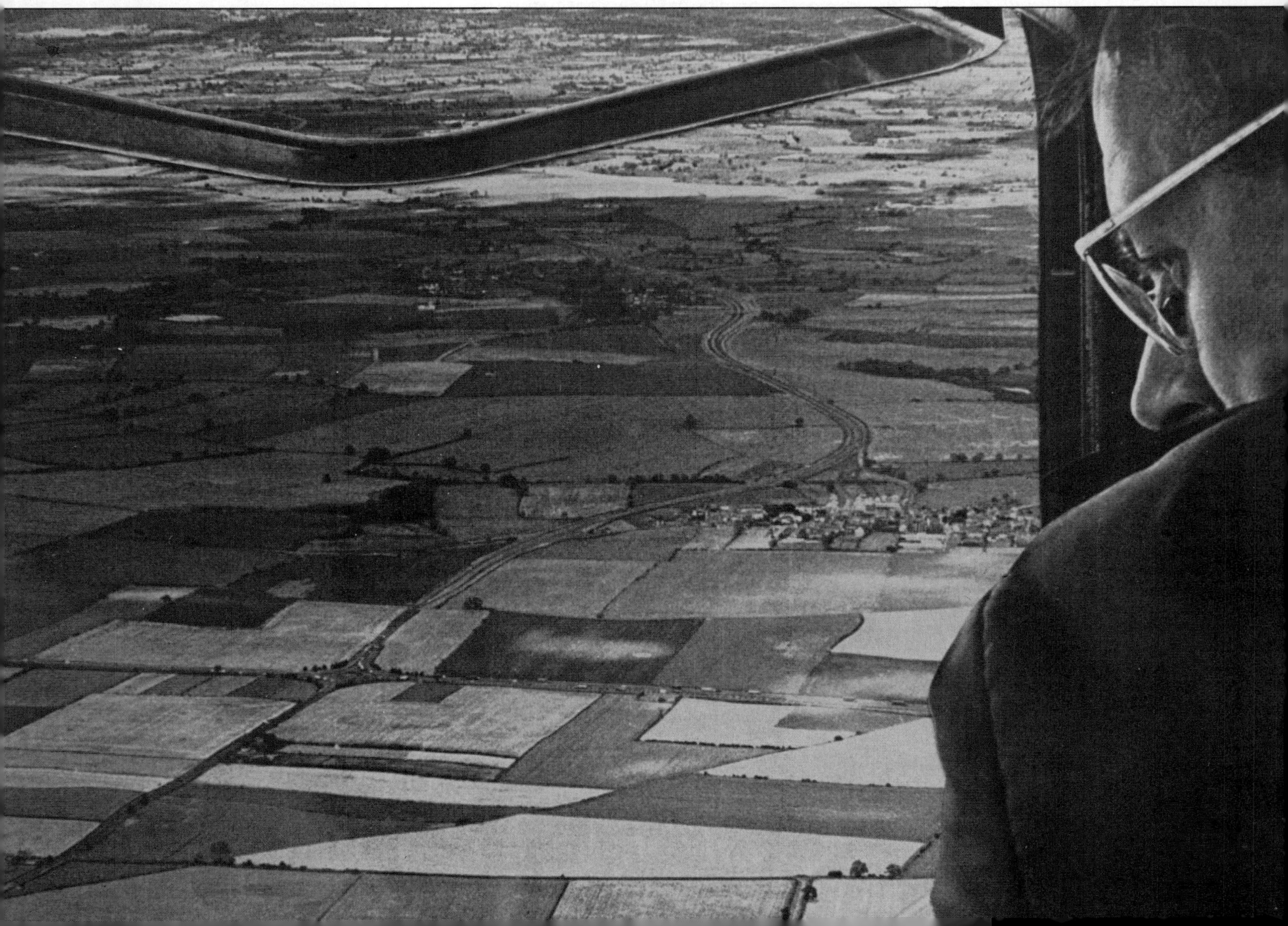

latter makes the very best camera platform of all. As my informant has photographed from the great pre-war rigids I bow, enviously, to his superior experience.

Before actually taking off, it is necessary to arrange a route and a routine with your pilot. If this is to be your first flight, do not try to do too much. Respect your pilot's experience with regard to restricted areas and altitudes. In general, with a 50mm lens and taking low-obliques (no horizon showing), an altitude of between 1000 and 1500 feet is about right. Try to circle your subject and decide on the best angle, then take several pictures. Use a kneepad to make an immediate note of each series. Ensure that the camera is set for a shutter speed of at least 1/500 sec and use masking tape to hold the lens set to infinity. Above all, make sure that no part of you or the camera touches the aircraft, other than feet and seat of course! A great aid to accurate viewfinding is a rubber eyecup for the viewfinder.

33. Southwell, Notts. Oblique picture from 5,000 feet.

If films have to be reloaded in the air be very careful, as it is very easy to put an exposed film back in the camera. Other than re-winding the leader right back into the cassette (a very bad procedure as it makes processing difficult as well as risking fogging the film) there is only one foolproof way to avoid this. As you take the exposed cassette out, bite off the leader before replacing it in the can. Keep exposed film in a right-hand pocket and unexposed in a left. The cardboard boxes should be discarded before leaving the ground.

Unless you have a lot of experience of interpreting air photographs it would be wiser to stick to recording the more obvious features revealed by buildings and earthworks. Crop and soilmarks can be very confusing for the inexperienced, and more than one revolutionary discovery has turned out to be the work of a playful tractor driver with a spare bag of fertilizer!

Processing aerial photographs is always a problem if you cannot do it yourself. After so much effort and expense it would be foolish to entrust the precious films to an amateur-orientated service. Purchase a copy of one of the more serious monthly photographic magazines and search the classified sections for the names of reputable laboratories. These are usually classified as 'professional' services, and their prices reflect this, but their work is far better than any high street developing and printing service. Alternatively, search your local Yellow Pages for professional photofinishing labs; you will be able to deliver and collect the films by hand and thus cut out the potential risk of sending the material through the post.

Regarding the actual printing of the monochrome, though 10x8ins is the smallest useful size, it does necessitate masking off a portion of the negative, so A4 would be better.

Finally, never be tempted to sell photographs of country houses, hotels, etc which you have passed over in your sorties. Not only does this undercut the professionals who try to make a living this way but, more importantly, it places at risk the private pilot's licence of your accomodating friend who make it all possible.

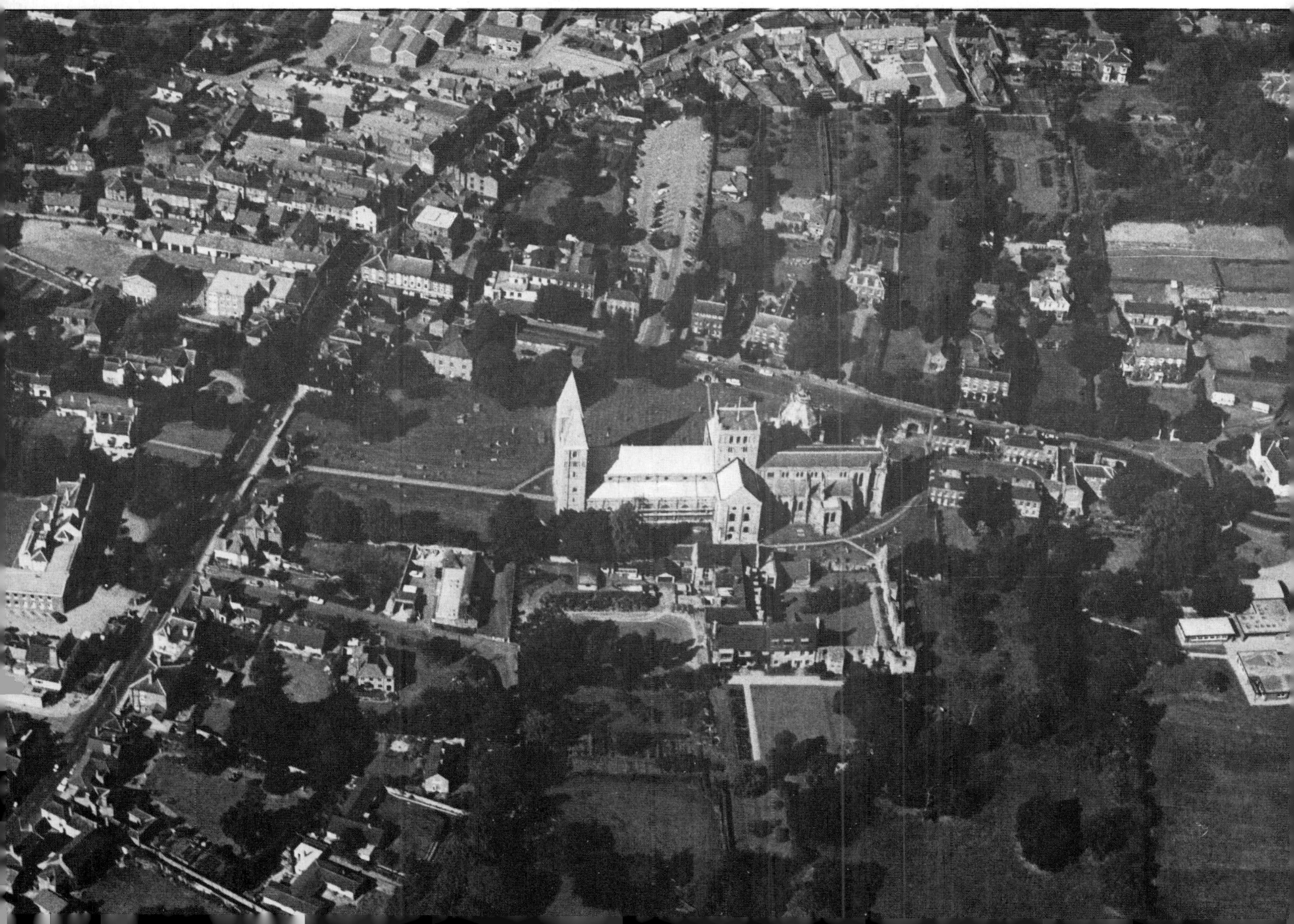

CHAPTER NINE

Basic Archaeological Photography

Archaeology is, of course, local history. Most active societies have a few members who assist on local digs. It goes without saying that the digging must be supervised by qualified and experienced people and that one of these will be a competent photographer. Nevertheless, local amateur back up is valuable both to the expert (who need worry less about mis-processing and other hazards) and to the local historian who will have his/her own record. Only by assisting in this way will the amateur build up experience in this vital but undervalued aspect of our craft. Do not be reticent about asking to take pictures. For many years there has been an unwritten convention in British archaeology that helpers can take their own photographs as long as they do not use them for commercial purposes, or publish them in any way without the permission of the site director.

Site photography is a specialised branch of the wider craft of historical photography. It can add numerous valuable skills which can be applied in many other local history situations. Equipment required is pretty basic, but should include a sturdy tripod, two camera bodies (for mono and colour), a selection of lenses and a separate exposure meter. As skill develops a set of filters can be added, consisting of yellow, green and red for mono work and polarizing for colour. System filters like Cokin are much more convenient than separate ones for each lens, and much cheaper too. Non photographic equipment should include half-inch paint brushes, old teaspoons, wooden lolly sticks and some dental instruments. These can be begged from a member of the profession.

34. A high viewpoint is best for stone structures.

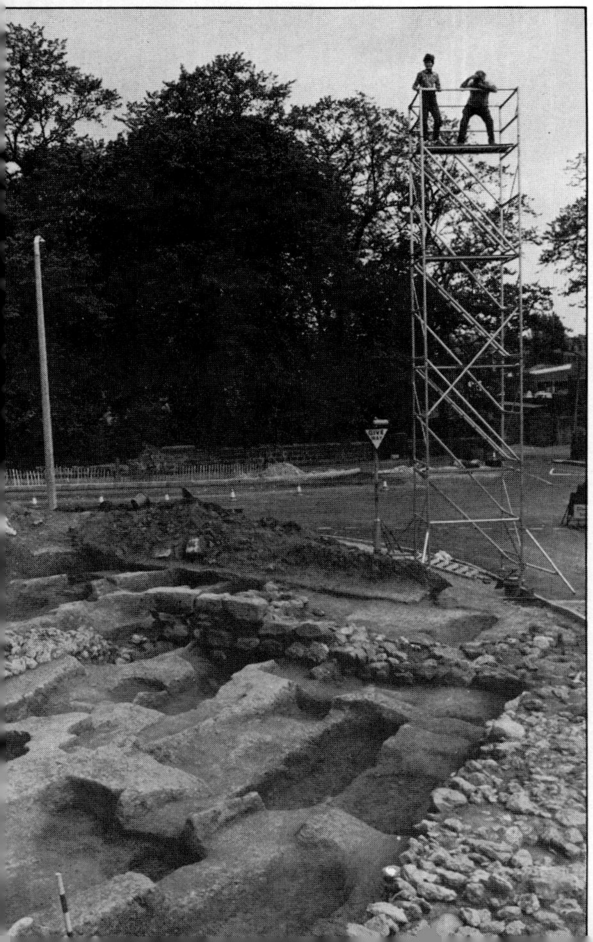

Because the official photographs are part of the permanent archive of the excavation they are usually taken in monochrome because of the superior keeping qualities. Colour is important, but chiefly as lecture illustrations and museum display material. For publication the printers will require 10in x 8in or A4 glossies. The amateur helper can safely leave this aspect in the hand of the official site photographer and go his/her own way, which usually means using slide film. For a summer dig, choose a fine-grained, warm-toned 100 ISO film, and in winter opt for the 400 ISO stock from the same manufacturer. Slide film, or *reversal film* as it is correctly known, has very little latitude for exposure errors, so that care must be exercised if the results are to be usable. Not very long since, in a definitive series of articles on modern archaeological site photography, I stated that the built-in exposure meters in automatic cameras are not capable of giving correct exposure of archaeological subjects. Recently I had the opportunity to check this fact for myself, during a winter rescue excavation of a possible mediaeval cemetery. For safety, I took photographs in pairs, using the auto setting and then the manual setting alternately. In the vast majority of cases the slides were identical, and even in the pictures where they were not, both slides were usable. I would therefore advise the tyro to use the automatic facilities for subjects which appear to have a reasonable distribution of lights and darks, but to use the *AE Lock* to fix in a setting from a more average portion of the subject, if the feature being photographed is predominantly dark or light. If using colour negative film, the automatic setting can safely be used all the time, as this type has an enormous exposure latitude.

The late M B Cookson (Sir Mortimer Wheeler's chief photographer) once said that cleanliness was the key to good site photography. Though equipment, materials and even excavation techniques have all changed radically in the thirty years since his death, his advice is still apposite. Whatever the subject, meticulous cleaning is necessary before the actual exposure. This can be ignored, but never eliminated, by careful and accurate excavation. Sides must be kept vertical as they are dug; baulks must be kept clear of spoil as they are used; edges between vertical and horizontal areas must be maintained as sharp angles and not allowed to deteriorate into curves. This cleaning for photography is usually begun with handbrushes and continued with paint brushes, teaspoons and even lolly sticks. Faint soil colours are emphasised by damping, whilst careful scraping can enhance line and textures. There is usually plenty of time, so care and thought can be given to the best possible presentation of the subject.

Few archaeological photographs are taken without a scale of some kind. Not only does this provide a reference for instant appraisal by the viewer, but it also makes it possible for a computer to extrapolate actual measurements from the pictures. The photographer should have a selection of scales available, as already discussed in chapter five. My practice of stencilling the unit of measurement on the scales becomes even more necessary, as in many archaeological subjects the scale is the only reference point; anyone who has had to work with old excavation pictures will endorse this. Many sites are extremely muddy, so some form of protection is needed for scales. My own are kept in a cloth bag which once held a projection screen. The bag shields the scales from the worst of the mud, and also doubles as a cloth to wipe them clean with when they have been used.

Situations

Stonework. On Roman and mediaeval sites, stonework is common. Naturally this must be meticulously cleaned with trowels and brushes, making sure that all soil is removed from between the joints. Most record photography of such subjects is done under diffused illumination, but consider using oblique sunlight to emphasise texture. Scales must be arranged so that at least one is vertical and one horizontal. It is the convention that the horizontal scale be parallel to the bottom and top frame edges.

Horizontal Surfaces. Most excavations today uncover reasonably large areas of ancient surface. These tend to be pitted with foundation trenches, post holes, and storage/rubbish pits. Photography is best from a high viewpoint, which can vary from a proper tower, on professional sites, to a stepladder, on amateur sites. One of the best which I have used has been a ladder lashed to two scaffold poles to form

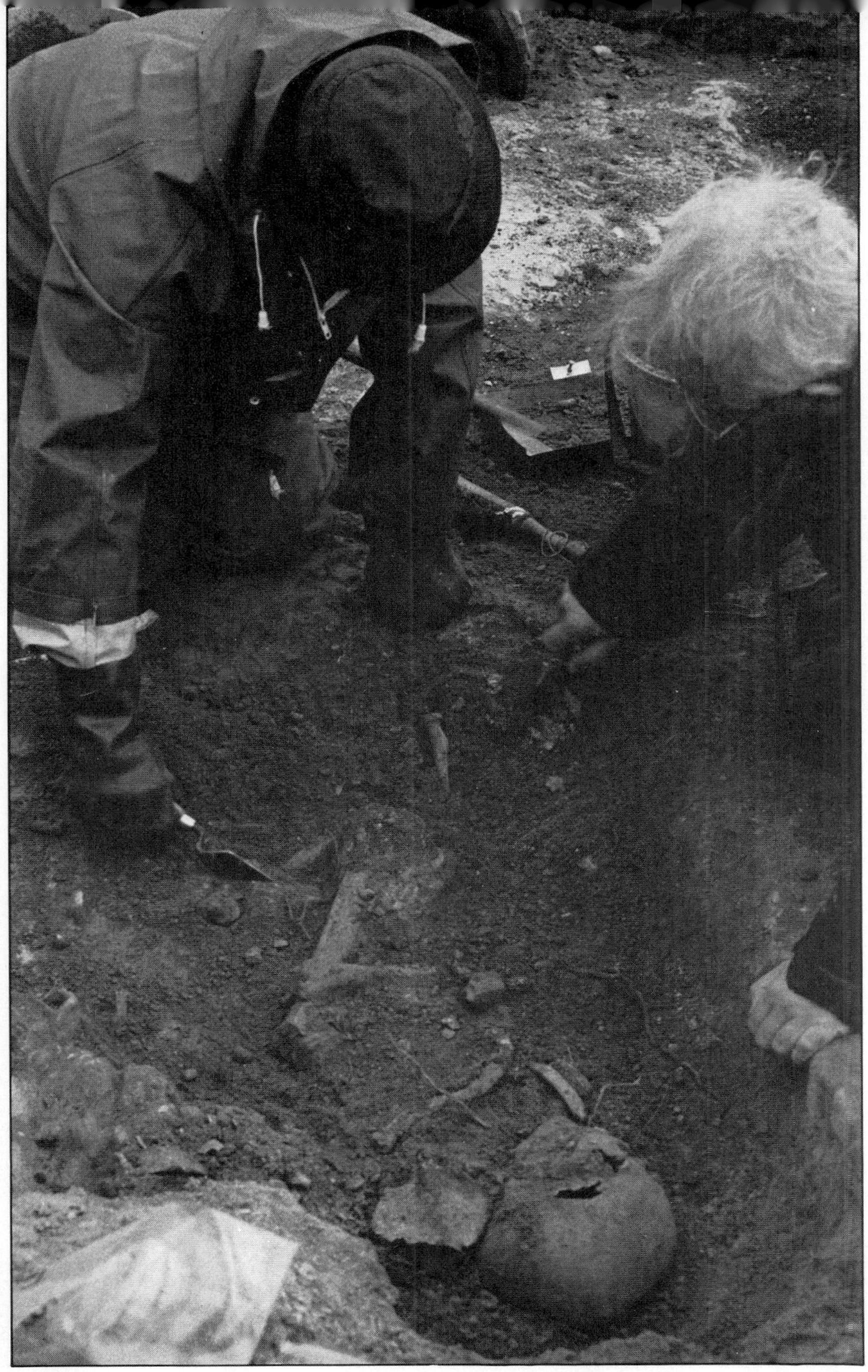

an extremely strong tripod. I have also used the upstairs of a derelict house which forms a good, but risky, perch. The best lighting is usually diffused sunlight coming towards the camera, necessitating an efficient lens hood. Scales should be distributed in such a way that some are parallel to the bottom and top frame edges, with some plumbed upright too. Remember always to ask permission before walking on cleaned surfaces.

Sections. Photography of earth sections needs special skills. It must always be done **after** the section has been drawn, as the preparation for photography involves emphasising strata in such a way as to make the section no longer an objective record. There are two ways to prepare the section. The easiest is simply to scrape a line with a trowel along each layer-junction so that a slight shadow is formed by the top-lighting which illuminates most sections. The best way is to undercut very slightly each layer junction, and to try in some way to emphasise the individual characteristics of each stratum, subtly roughening the texture of some layers and

35. Local society members must be prepared to turn out in all weathers to investigate and record chance discoveries.

36. Burials are photographed from vertically above. This example was discovered on a rescue site and cleaned very quickly.

39. Casual investigation of a building site in Castleford in 1965 produced cremated bird bones in a Romano-British pot. Twenty years later, archaeologists found other evidence which suggested that a Mithraic temple stood on the site. This photograph, after two decades, became important corroborative evidence. Moral; file negatives and prints carefully.

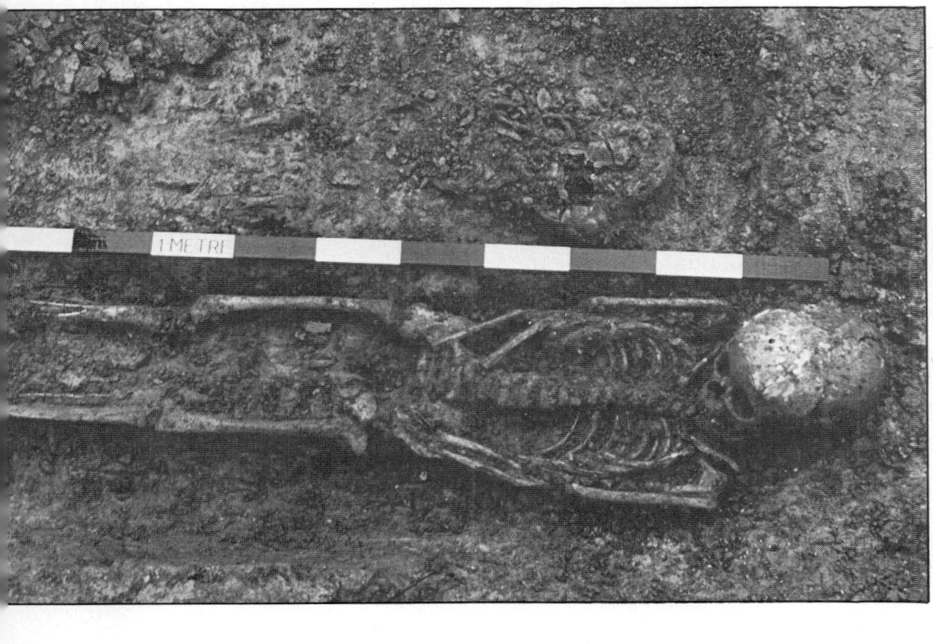

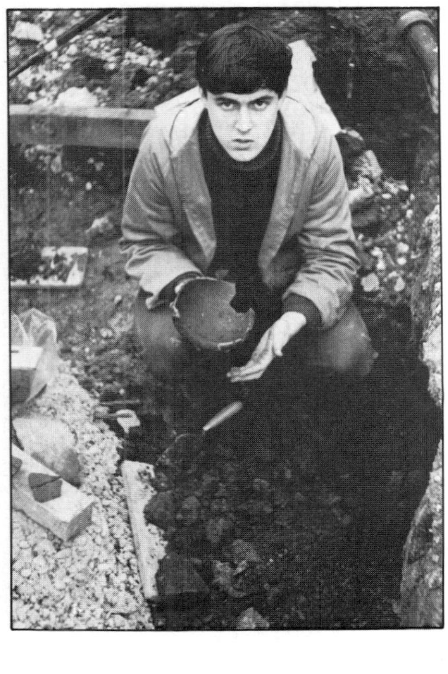

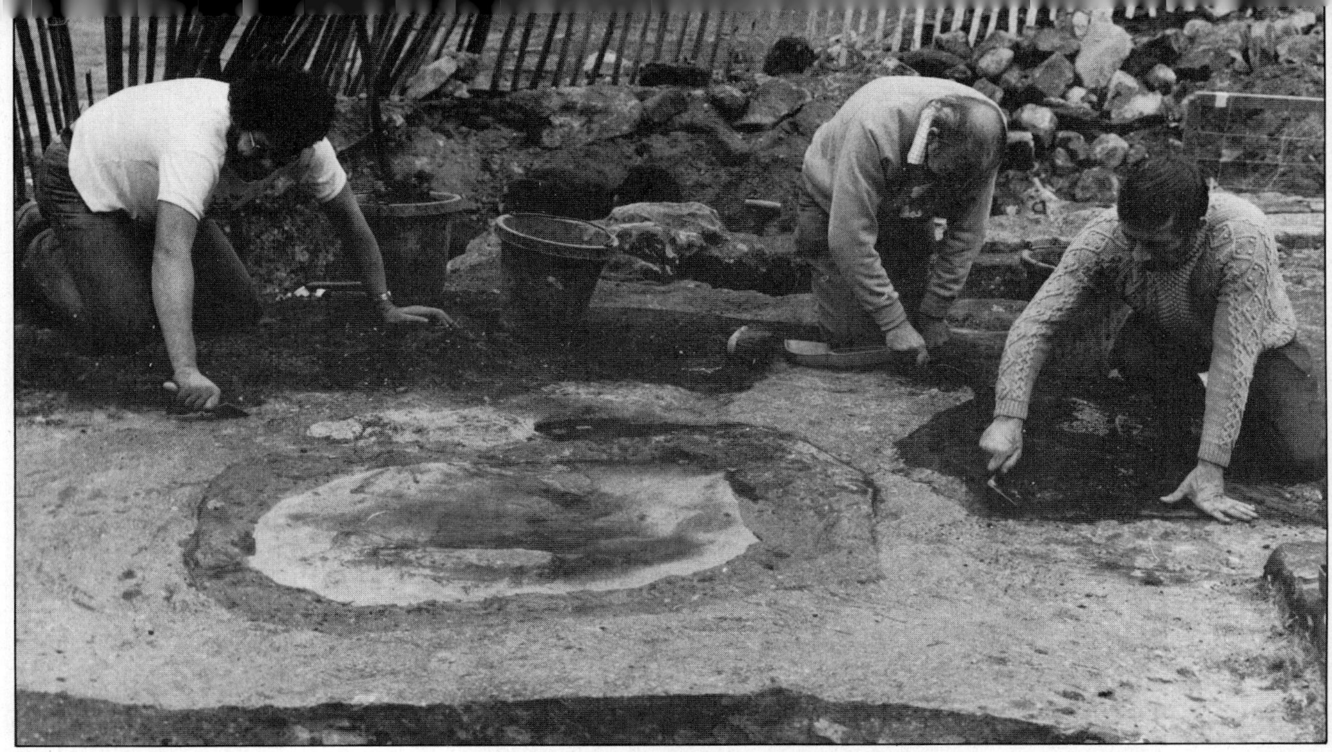

smoothing others. All stones must be carefully scraped around, and hair-roots must be cut gently, so that no soil is dislodged.

Filters for photographing sections must be chosen with care. If using monochrome remember that whilst a filter will darken one colour, it will also lighten another. some sections benefit from the use of a *polarizer* when using colour.

Pits. Pits vary tremendously in depth. Whether they are half-sectioned (dug so that there is a baulk down the centre which can be drawn and photographed) or totally emptied, a scale must be placed vertically in the pit to indicate depth. When bottom details must be shown and there is insufficient light at the bottom, then judicious use of flash is necessary. A tripod is vital for this, and bracketing is necessary unless you have one of the cameras which can read a combination of flash and ambient light straight off the film.

Graves. Burials vary enormously from period to period. The ones most often met with on excavation sites are Roman, Saxon and mediaeval. Though the majority which survive are inhumations, plenty of cremations are also found. The latter can be either in containers, or not, though it is generally evident that the ashes were originally in some container of organic material, like a leather bag which has subsequently decayed. Careful cleaning is important for cremations, especially those which have been partially scattered by later agriculture. It is then simply a matter of placing a suitable scale in position and photographing from vertically above.

Inhumations are always photographed from vertically above, though on very muddy sites this often necessitates the use of an extremely wide angle lens with its inevitable distortions. A one metre scale is always sufficient for adult and child burials, though tiny babies need one of twenty centimetres. If a complete cemetery is being dug, then a small blackboard about twenty centimetres square is needed. On this can be written the grave number and other relevant details. Some writers have advocated the use of white plastic letters for this purpose, but I feel that they have never actually used them when standing in thick mud which is slowly freezing in the wind! Chalk is much better, and can be erased easily by wiping the complete data-board on the trousers.

Historians are now getting information on the frequency of death at different seasons of the year by a careful analysis of the orientation of individual graves in Saxon and mediaeval cemeteries.

37. Cleaning for photography involves careful scraping until all loose material is removed.

Before the invention of the compass, east was found by lining up poles at sunrise. Naturally, this would produce a variation towards north in winter and the south in summer. Site photographers provide the research data by placing a white PVC arrow on the data board in each grave of a Christian cemetery, and align it to magnetic north with a good

40. Metric scale, of the type described in the text, used for an oblique picture of a Saxon Christian grave, excavated in advance of road works.

41. Flash can be useful, as in this case of a late Saxon skeleton. Note the lettered scale.

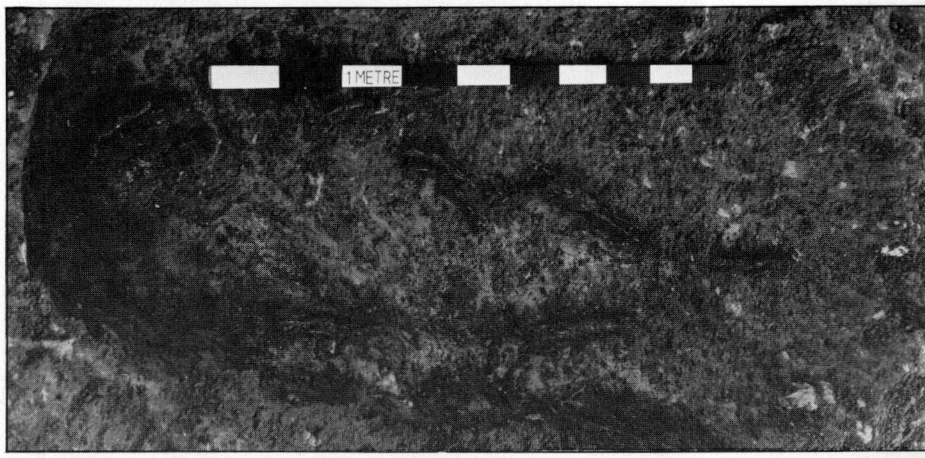

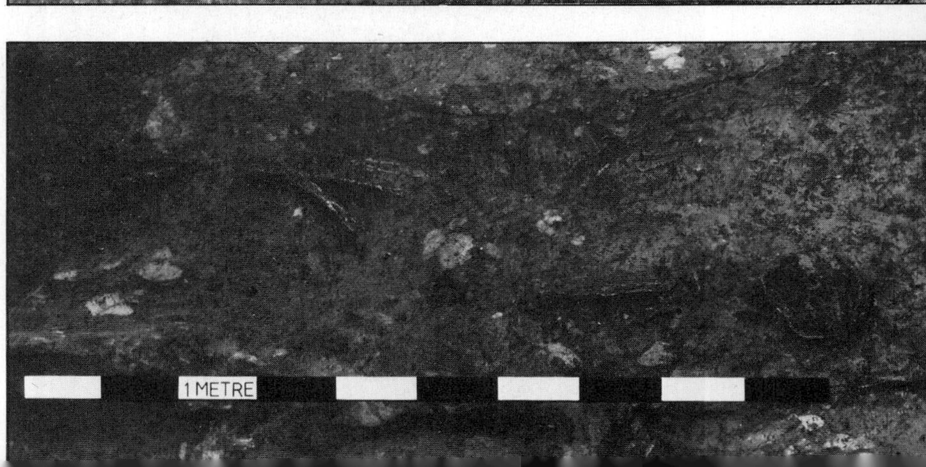

compass, ensuring that no iron or steel tools are close. This practice is also of value in non-Christian cemeteries to fix the often arbitrary orientation of each grave.

Work around the site. Though not strictly speaking archaeological photography, it is useful and important to take pictures of people at work around the site. As slides these shots fill out lectures and gratify the helpers who appear on them. As prints they form useful publicity material for local newspapers, and excellent illustrations for books. Both help to show later researchers that the dig was conducted in a proper scientific manner and that the conclusions reached were valid ones in the light of the evidence. As the years pass, these pictures assume greater personal value, especially as many of the people on them move away, grow old, or die.

This chapter has formed a very basic introduction to archaeological photography. By following it the local history photographer will not appear entirely gauche on a site. Reading it does not qualify a person to take over the photography of a dig. Only experience, together with the reading of the books and articles in the bibliography, can go some way towards imparting this qualification.

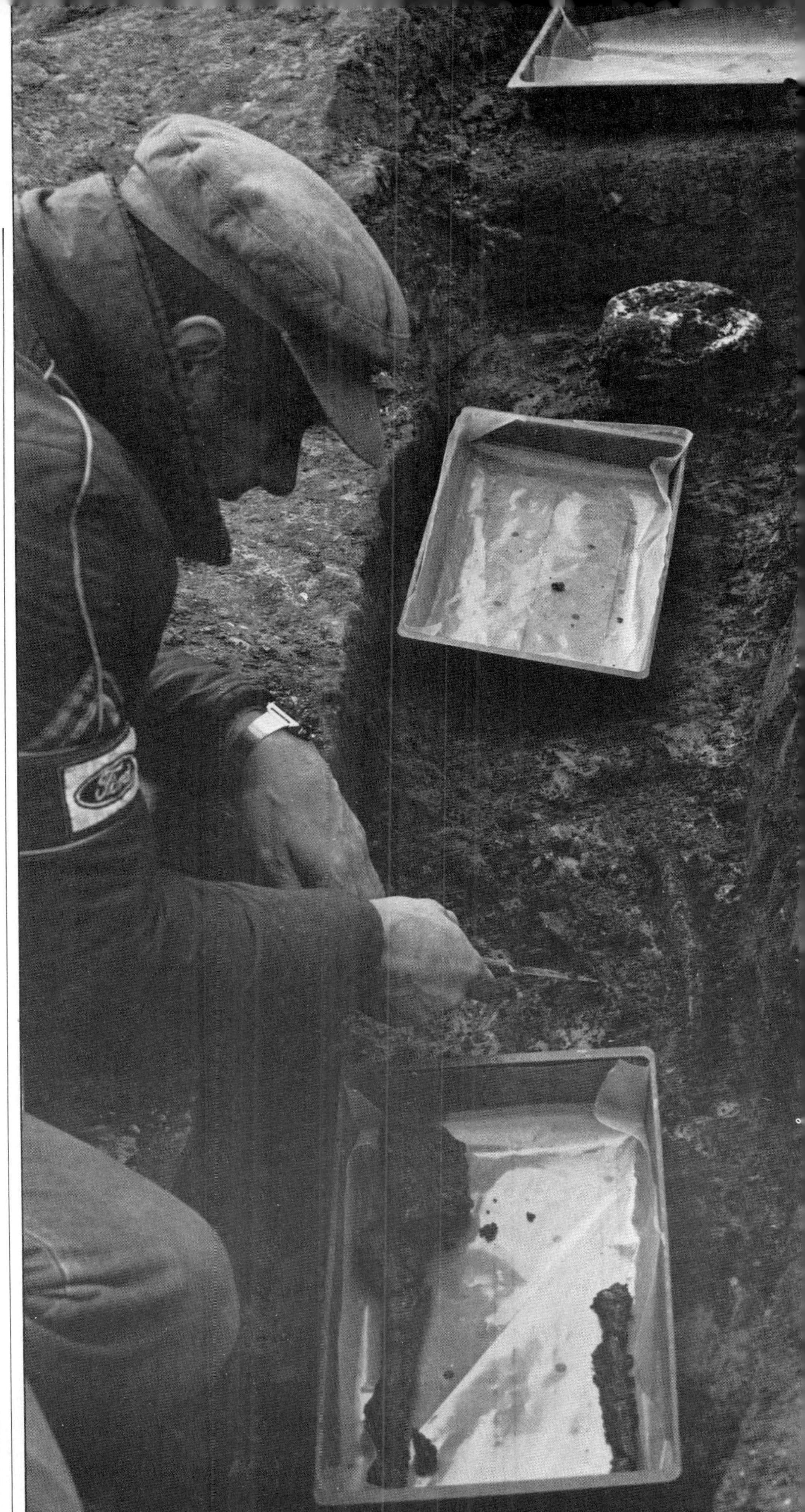

38. A people type picture, useful for publicity and as society history. In this case we were finishing the excavation of a complex site in advance of development. In its final stage the dig became a race against time and weather. Here we see a chilled member trying to lift the extremely friable remains of a Saxon skeleton in temperatures well below zero. The white patina on the skull is, in fact, frost!

CHAPTER TEN

Photography in Industrial Archaeology

Many historians refuse to acknowledge industrial archaeology as a valid field of study. Most archaeologists too would have reservations, so it may be useful to examine these problems before actually discussing the role of photography in industrial archaeology, if indeed there is such a thing!

I think it would be fair to say that the term **archaeology** was appended to the study of this aspect of the industrial revolution for the same reason that it has, more recently, been appended to the study of crashed aeroplanes from the Second World War. Both early students of industry and aeroplanes approached their data-base by digging. To the uninformed, archaeological excavation is just that; digging! Therefore, the more respectable term 'archaeology' was added to the names of both activities. Both real historians and real archaeologists realise that the terminology is based upon a simplistic idea of archaeological excavation, but the names seem to have stuck.

At the present time industrial archaeologists appear to be trying to approach the standards of real archaeologists in their unearthing, if not yet their recording, of early sites, so eventually the pastime may achieve validity. Unfortunately, the finds-based approach of the so-called aircraft archaeologists leaves them a much longer road to travel before they achieve respectability.

Accepting then that industrial archaeology can be a valid field of study, what contribution can photography make? It needs little thought to realise that photography can play as vital a part as a recording medium as it does in conventional historical photography. Having realised this, it has to be accepted that the often peculiar conditions of industrial archaeology demand some modifications of the techniques discussed in previous chapters.

Equipment is largely the same as for conventional historical work, but as much industrial archaeology recording is done in artificial light, several powerful flashguns become a necessity. Damp, too, is more prevalent in industrial sites, and this has a most unfortunate effect on electronic flashguns. Experience suggests that the effects of damp can be minimised or eliminated by the use of WD40, a proprietry moisture-proofer used chiefly on damp car ignition parts!

Because of the nature of most industrial sites, faster film than usual is advocated, and it would be sensible to standardise on ISO 400 stock for both monochrome and colour. Sometimes the photographs may be the only record, in which case priority must be given to the monochrome photographs because of their archival stability.

The local historian's first encounter with industrial archaeology will very likely be when he/she is called upon to record a local watermill or windmill. For obvious reasons old flour milling buildings are extremely dusty, and the dust is also quite explosive, so never use a naked flame when trying to clean up preparatory to photography. Indeed, in my experience, the dust is so choking and penetrating that it is wiser to leave photographic equipment in the boot of the car until the dust of cleaning has settled; this can take up to a couple of days!

Having reached this stage, the experienced local historical photographer wonders where to place the scales. The answer is, back in the car! Proper scales always look out of place in old mills, and for some years I have chosen to use members of the recording team as living scales.

One problem is to record machinery which was designed to move in a still picture. There are two possible answers to this. The easiest way is to use a powerful electronic flash on its auto setting to completely freeze the motion of, say, a waterwheel. The other way is to use a tripod and make a time exposure which will show the moving machinery as a blur. Neither method is completely satisfactory, but a combination of the two sometimes works. You place the camera on a tripod and make a long time exposure of the moving parts, manually firing off an electronic flash during the exposure. This may have to be done several times to achieve one good picture, but eventually you should have a picture showing blurred motion, with, superimposed upon it, a ghost image of the parts frozen in action.

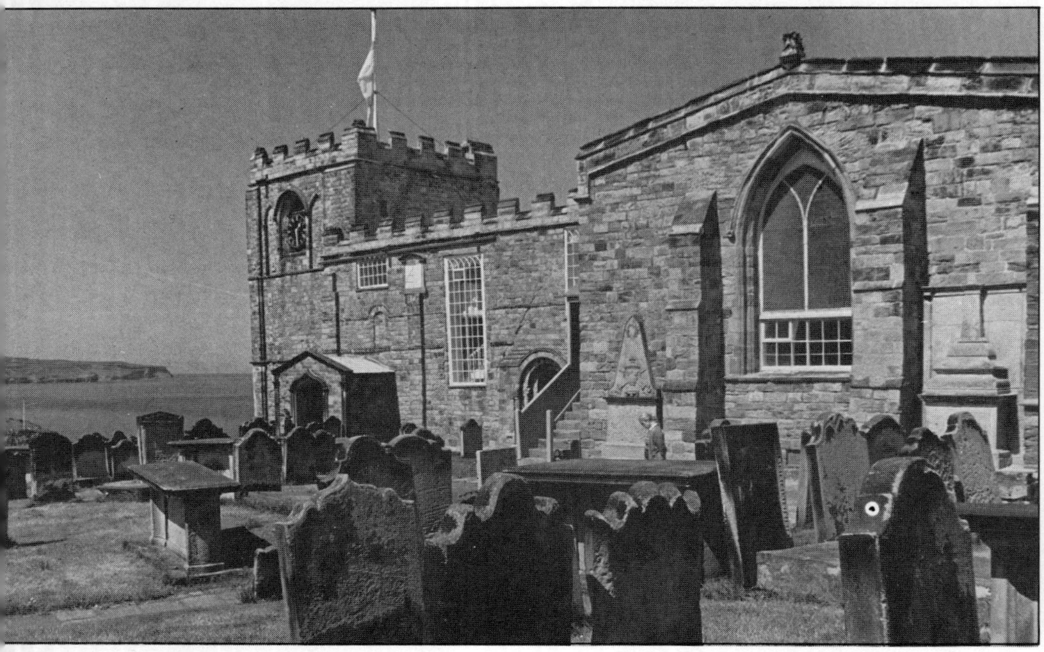

42. Whitby parish church, on the headland above the town. The orange filter darkens blue skies.

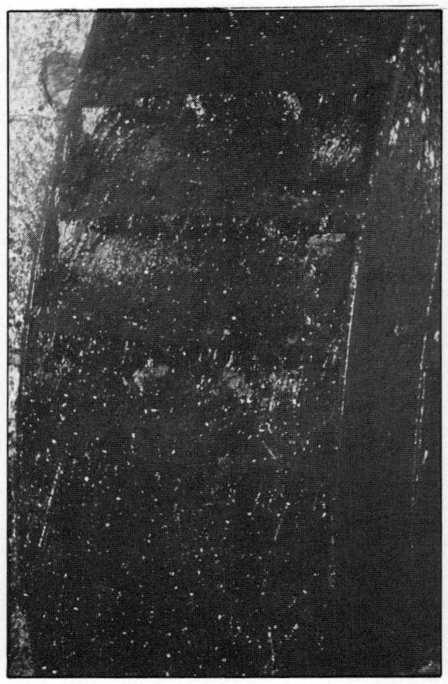

45. Overshot waterwheel pictured with electronic flash which has 'frozen' the movement and the water.

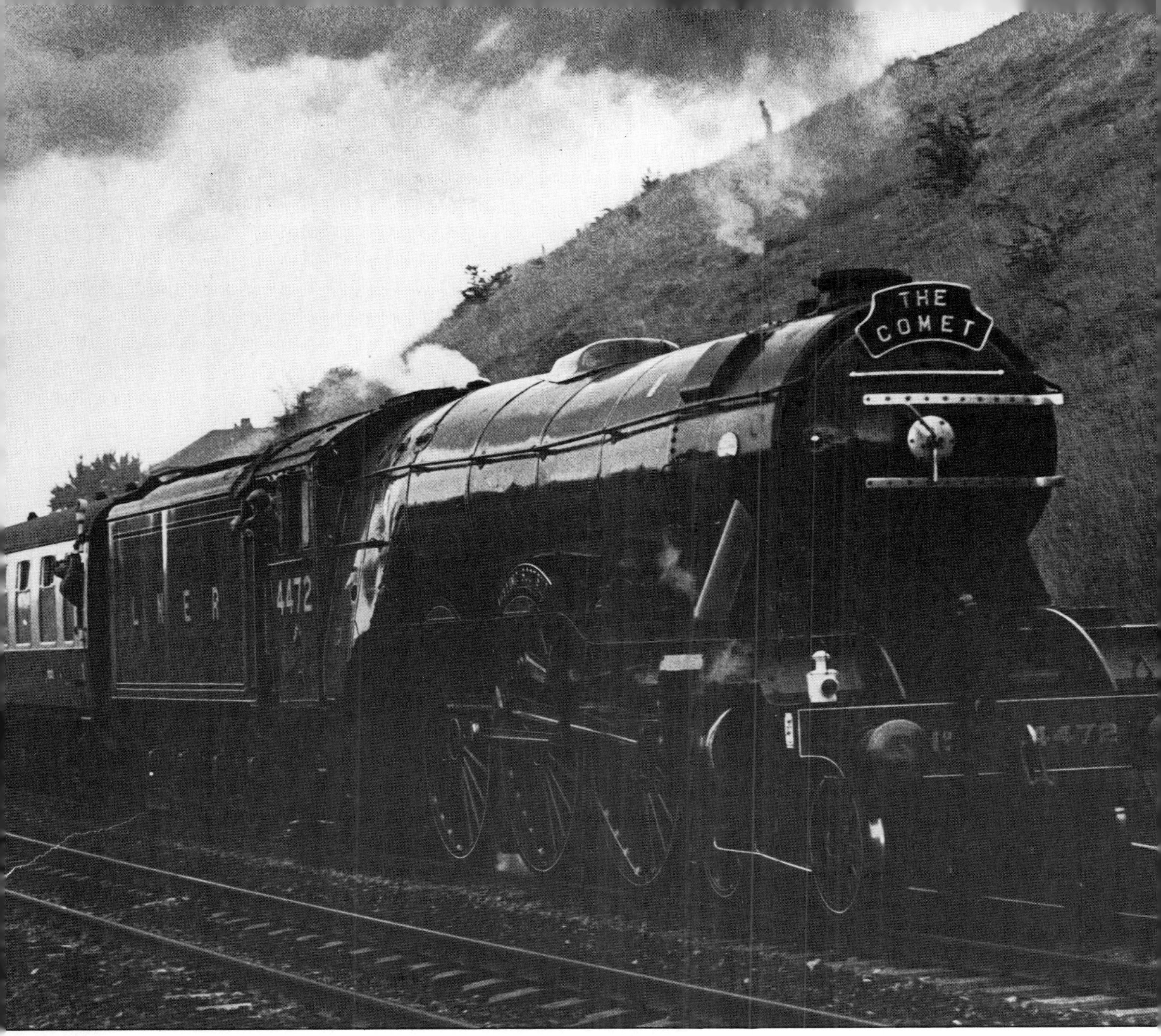

43. A restored locomotive at speed. A fast shutter speed is necessary to 'freeze' the motion.

Canals and railways come under the industrial heading, and there can be few districts without one or the other. Of the two, railways have always been photographed more often and even today the railway enthusiasts outnumber the canal enthusiasts both in numbers and in loquacity. Most enthusiasts tend to prefer photographing locomotives and narrow boats to recording stations and warehouses. Yet the latter are in the most danger, mainly because they are still in use and subject to alteration to make them more efficient. Whilst waiting for a train at my local railway station I noticed for the first time the splendid Victorian cast iron columns which hold up the roof. These have probably never been photographed. When I worked on another local station as a student a quarter of a century ago, the ticket office was exactly as it had been when the station was opened in the 1840s. I never got around to photographing it, and now it is long gone. My excuse is that at that time there was not the awareness that there is today, but I was aware and did nothing about it. I hope that you, my readers, are not only aware but take the necessary act on.

Now that some industrial archaeologists are beginning to look to conventional archaeology fcr excavation techniques, the time may not be far off when the advice in the last chapter, on archaeological photography, is equally valid for industrial sites. When that happens, industrial archaeology will have come of age.

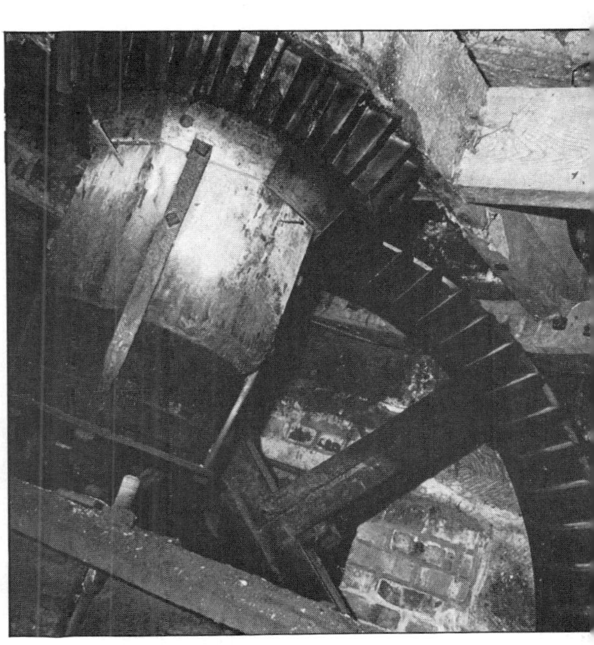

44. Automatic flash in the depths of a nineteenth century watermill. Even the 28mm wide-angle lens is insufficient to encompass the whcle mechanism.

CHAPTER ELEVEN

A Visual Notebook

My final chapter is really a celebration of the camera's chief advantage, its visual immediacy. Most photographs are taken in well under a hundredth of a second and really do freeze an instant in time. The annual outing of your local society can be recorded accurately, quickly and cheaply. A picture can record exactly who attended a particular meeting or conference. The Christmas decorations in the High Street can be compared over a period of years, or the games played in the playground of the infant school. All these things and many others are easily possible. It is my hope that this publication, the distillation of thirty years enthusiasm in local history, archaeology and photography, kindles in the reader a similar enthusiasm.

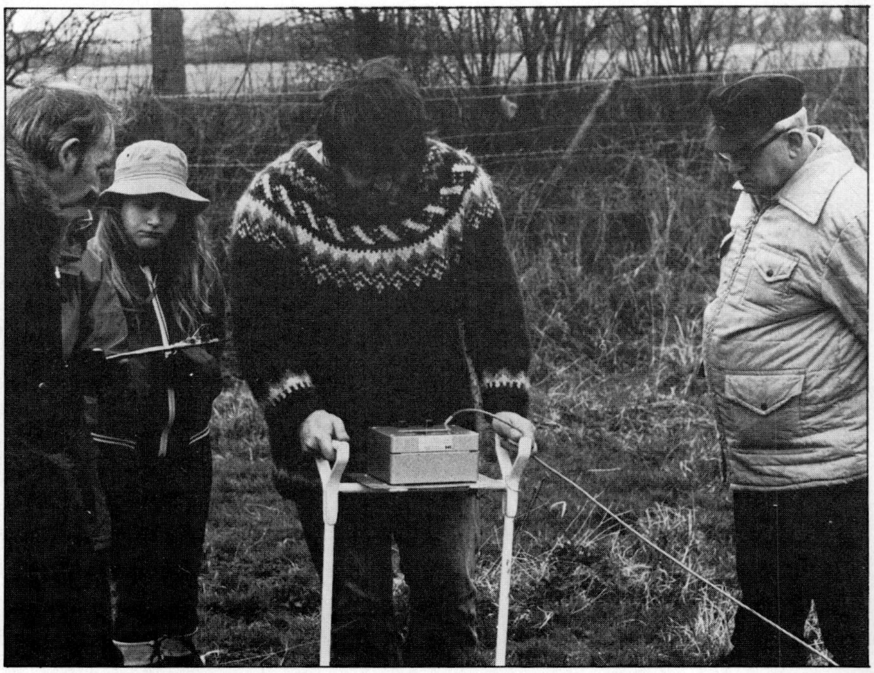

46. A geophysical survey in conjunction with Bradford University. The people involved will appreciate the picture in years to come.

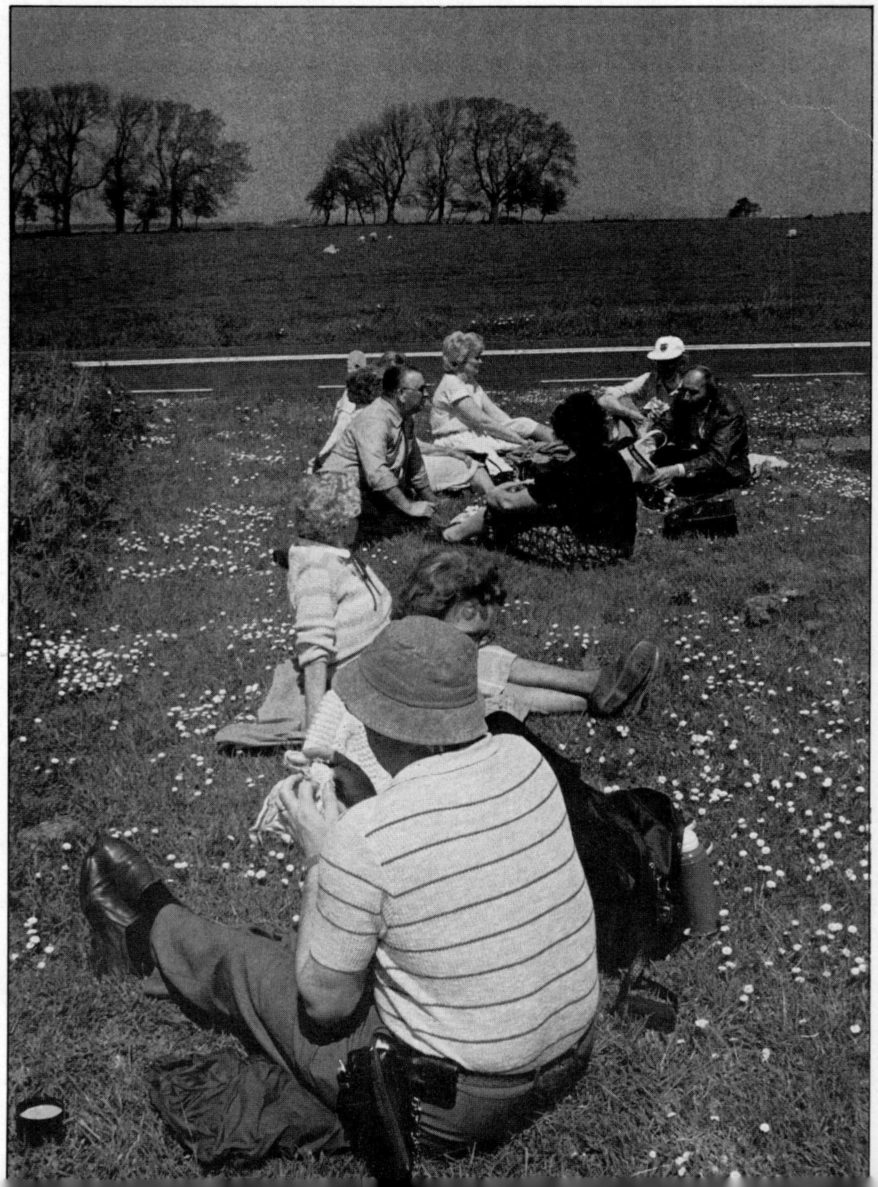

48. Picnic. Society outings by coach generate hundreds of good pictures. Here a group from my society picnic at Carrawburgh on Hadrian's Wall.

47. Investigatory group in a cellar. We were recording an old building before renovation and I had been shooting a lot of formal record pictures. I noticed that the group gathered around to examine something which had been found. A useful memory shot which, in its colour version, makes an excellent lecture illustration.

49. Industrial archaeology enthusiast. Sometimes the best angle for a picture involves a degree of contortion! As well as being a memory shot, this one makes a useful instructional aid. Have you recorded your cast iron street furniture yet?

50. A dig tends to bring out the personalities of the participants. Again, the sort of shot that makes memories and society history.

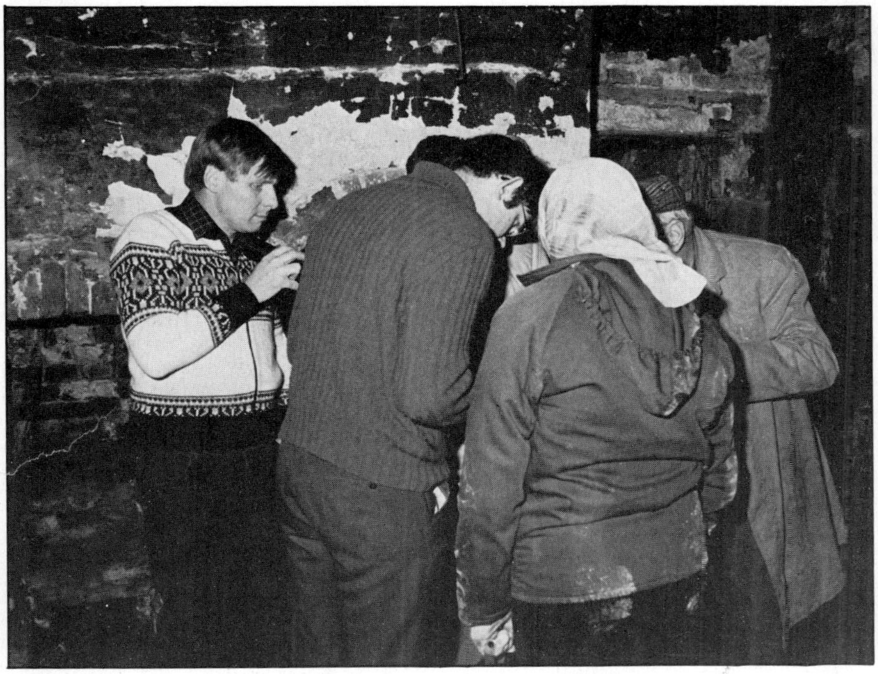

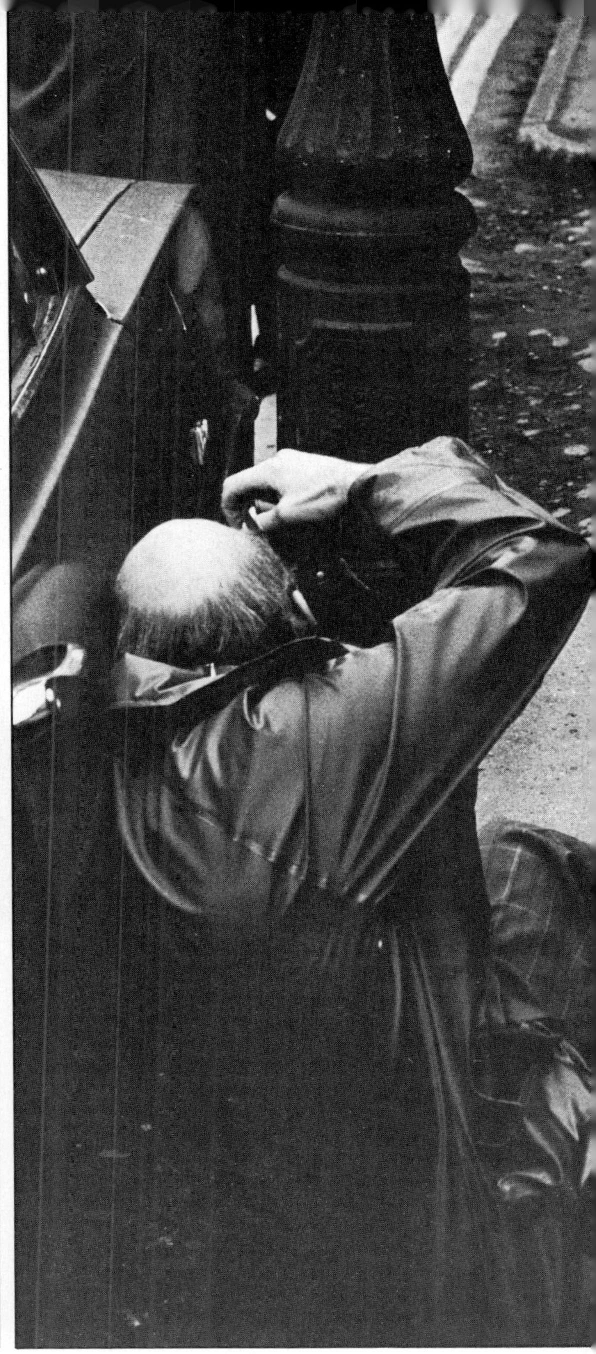

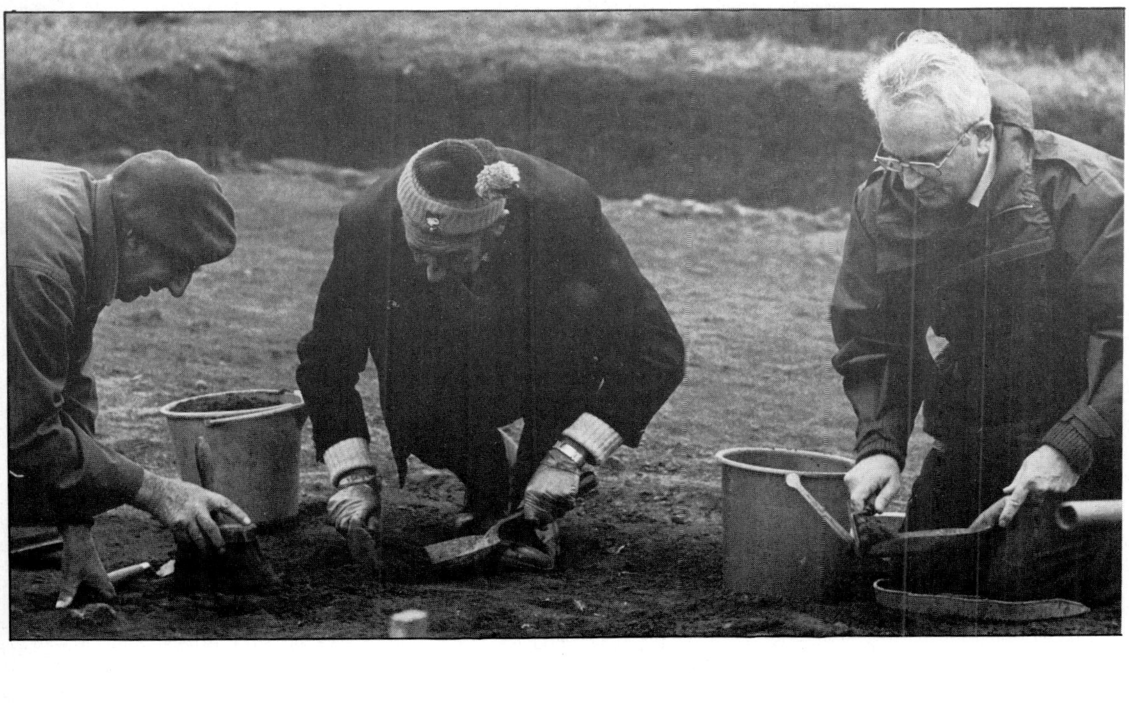

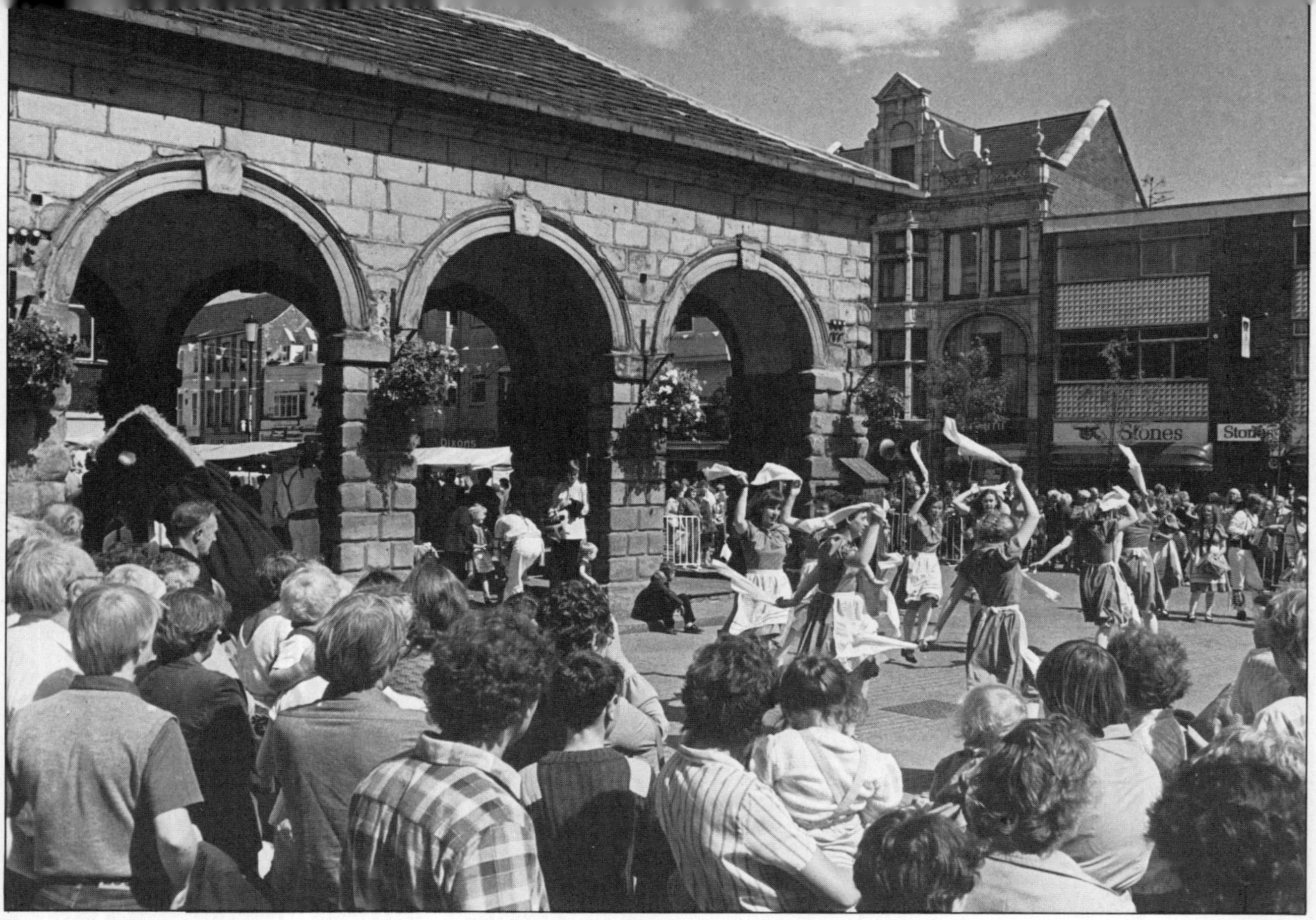

51. Folk dancing in summer. Taken from the back of the crowd and showing the crowd, the event and the surroundings.

52. Sunday afternoon on the Nidd, near Knaresbrough, Yorks.

53. Historic climate 'deviations' are well-worth recording. On this occasion, during one of the recent severe winters, I fastened a camera to the dashboard of my car, facing forwards. The focussing was set on infinity and the exposure set according to the lighting. Conditions were so close to 'white out' that I had to wait for other vehicles to obtain a picture with anything on it. Soon after this was taken, I had to dig out the driving wheels in appalling conditions and miles from anywhere. Sheer terror took over and I got no pictures! I should add that I had to go out, otherwise I would not have risked it.

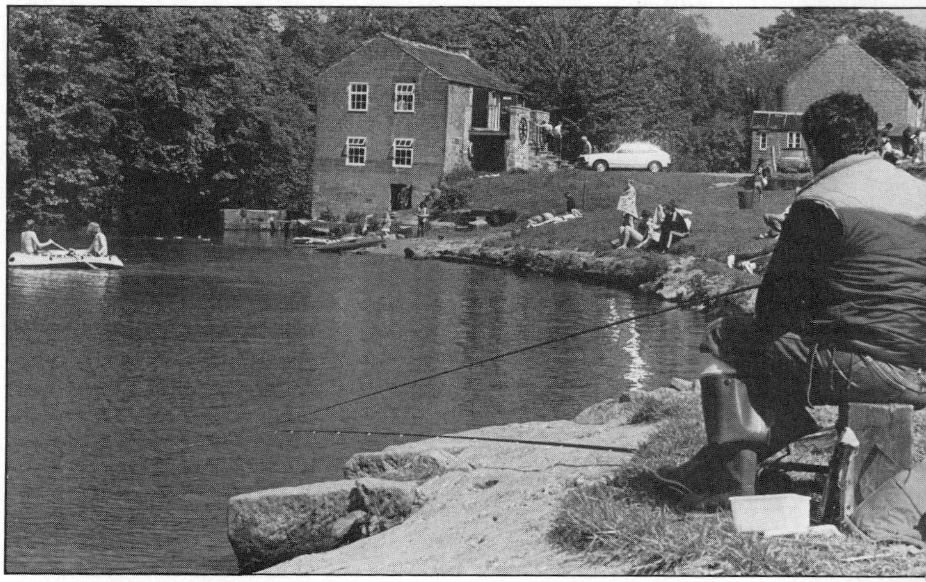

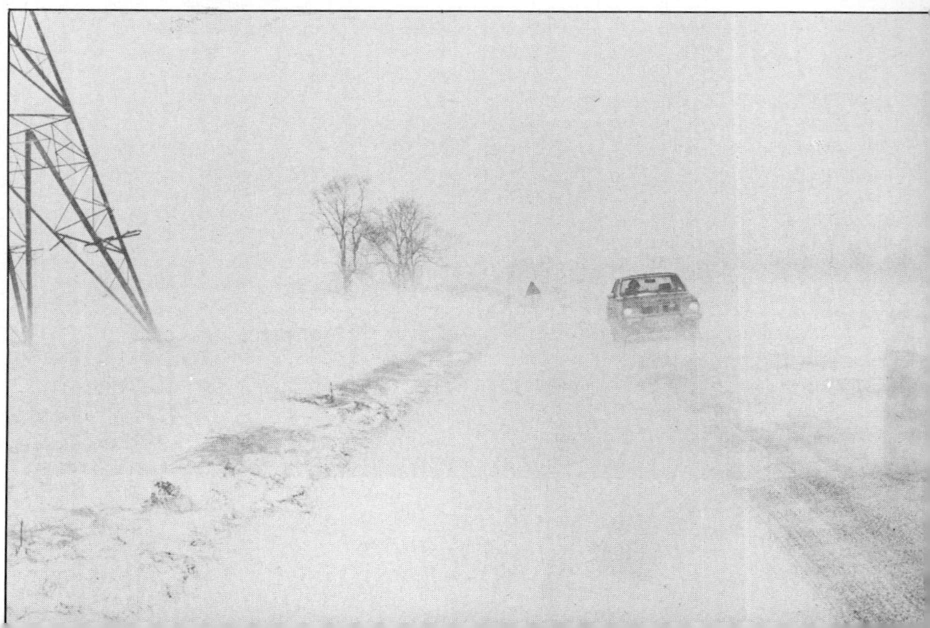

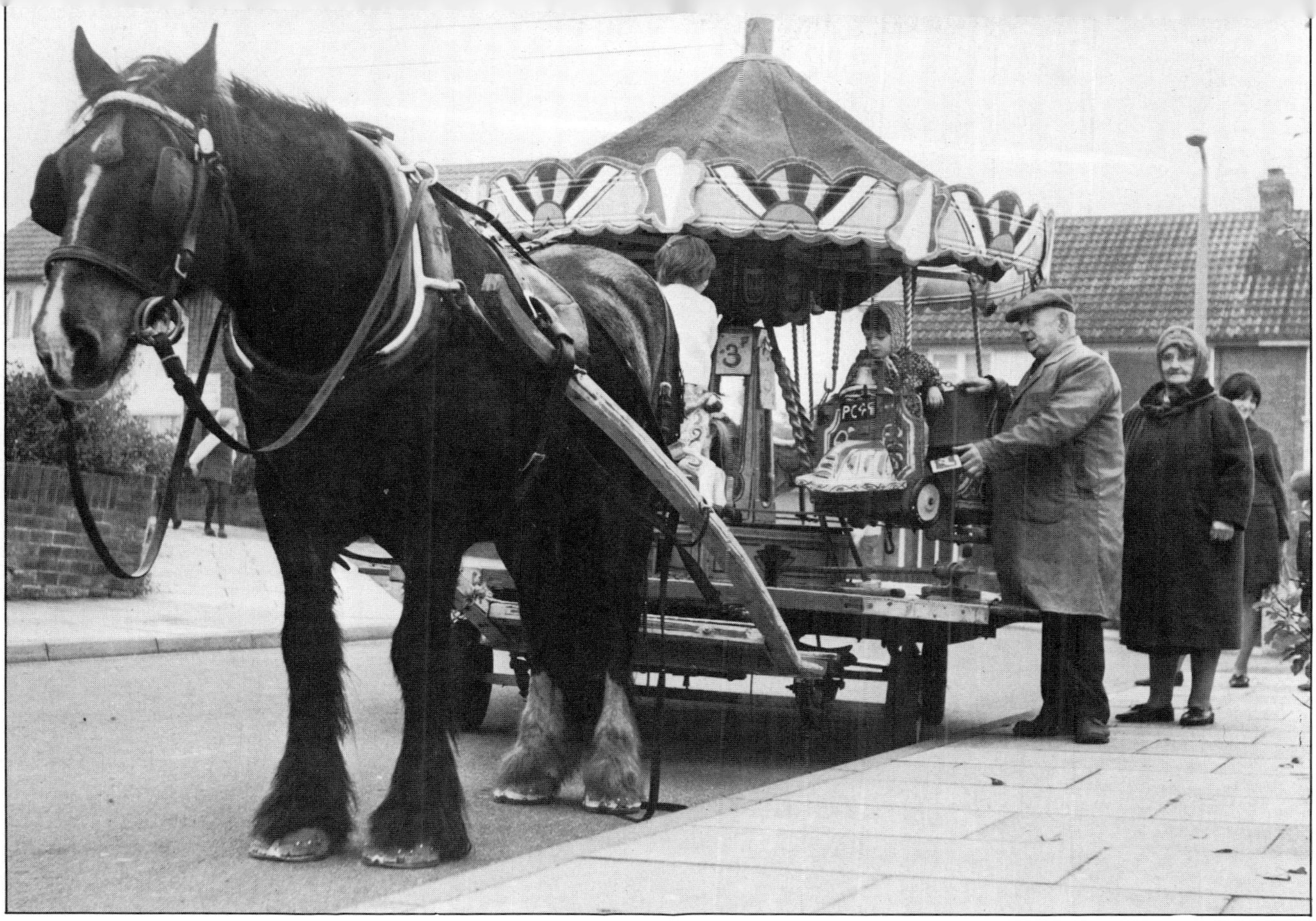

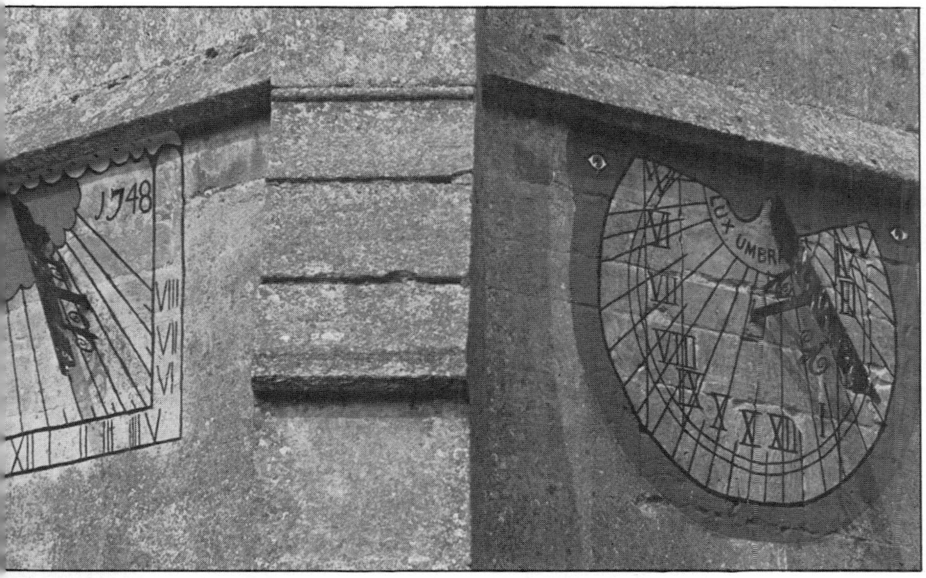

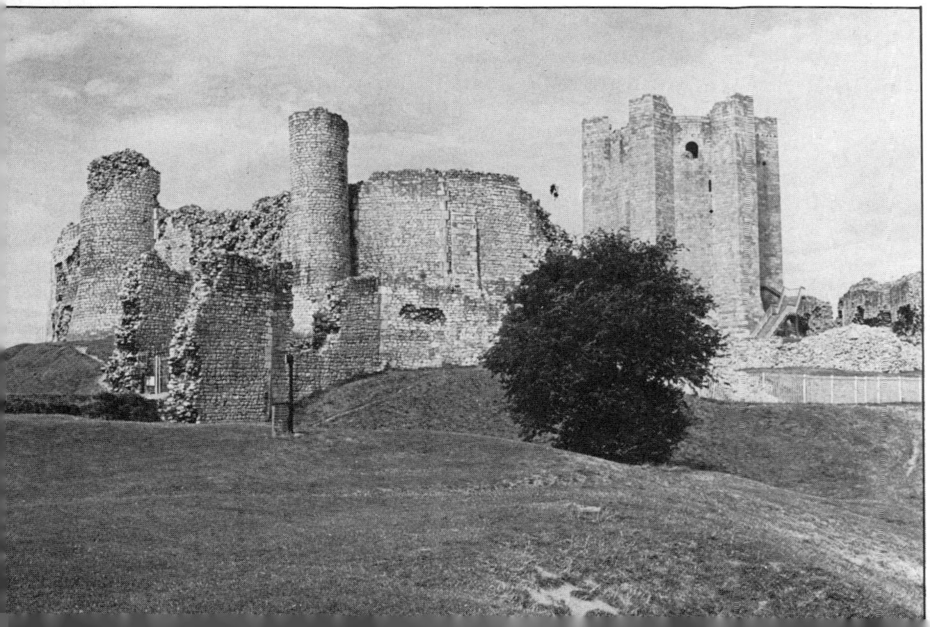

54. A horse-drawn roundabout pictured in 1971. This machine was a familiar sight around Castleford, Pontefract and district in my childhood, and obviously long before. Ideally, I should have shot it in a street of old terraced houses, but this opportunity presented itself whilst I was testing a 'new' used camera. Reproduced from a commercial print.

55. Sun-dials on the tower, Naunton Church, Glos.

56. Conisborough Castle. Ruined castles and abbeys are notoriously difficult to photograph in a meaningful way. Though several shots of details etc. should be taken, an overall view should also be attempted. Close features like trees can be used to either hide unwanted modern intrusions or to aid the composition.

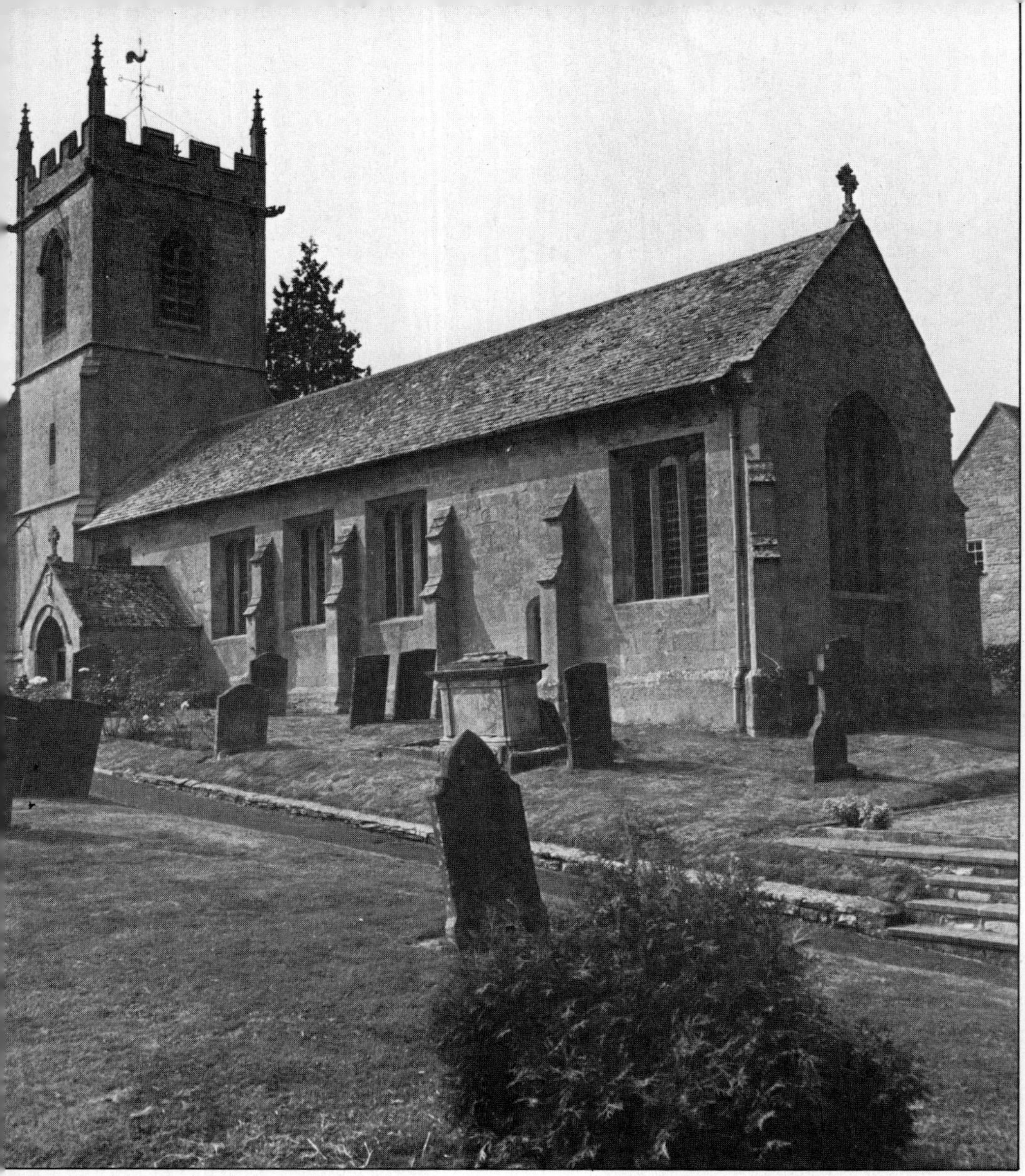

57. Naunton Church, Gloucestershire. Unless it is possible to move right back, some degree of tilting is necessary in order to include the whole tower. Use of a wide angle lens does help but produces an overlong foreground, which can be improved by the inclusion of a shrub or a gravestone. A telephoto lens, such as a 135mm, enables close-up detail to be pulled in without too much distortion.

58. Warkworth Castle, Northumberland.

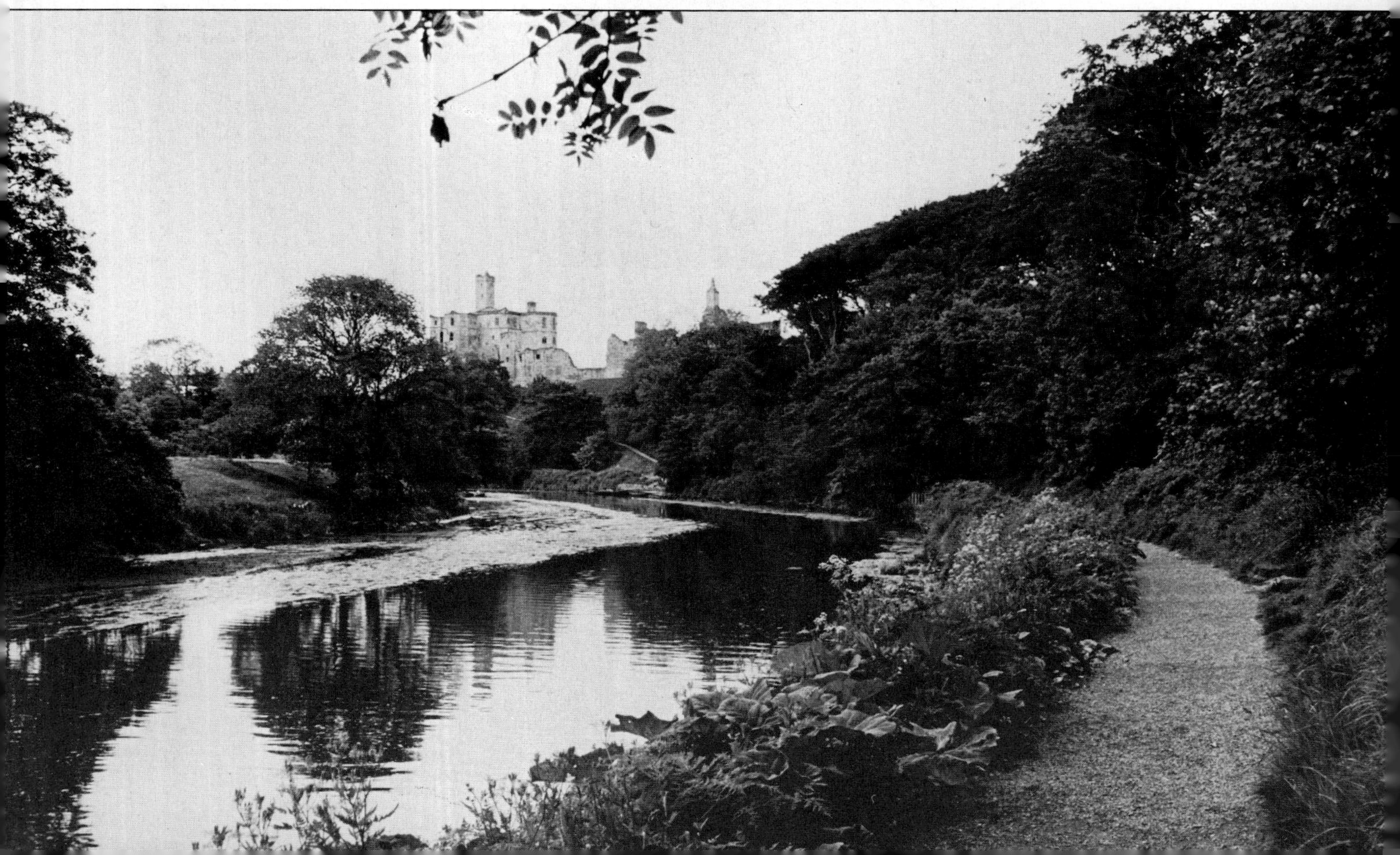

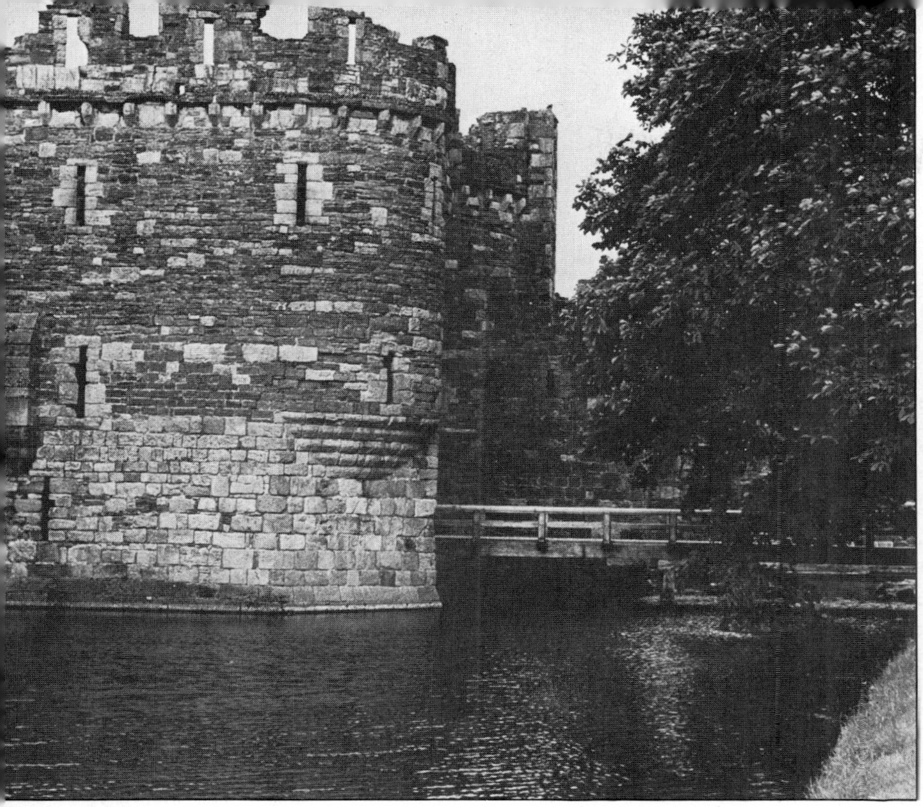

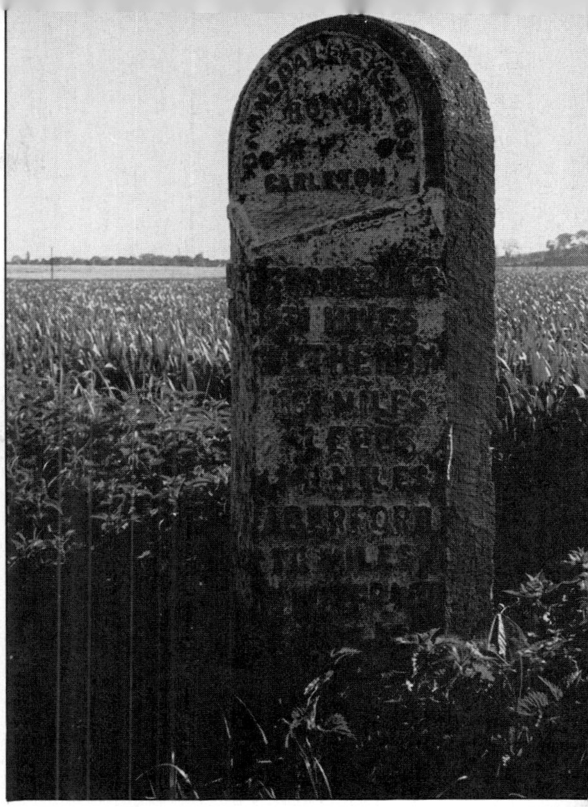

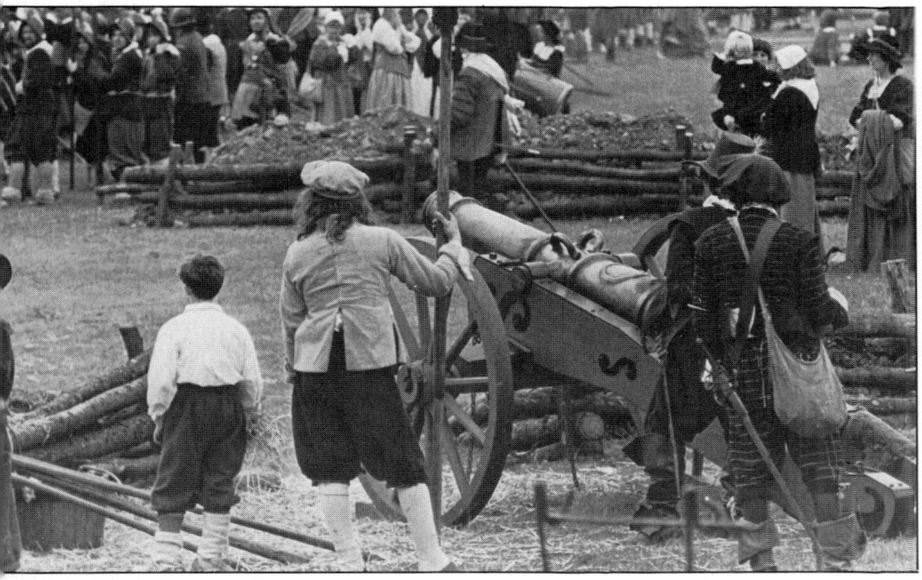

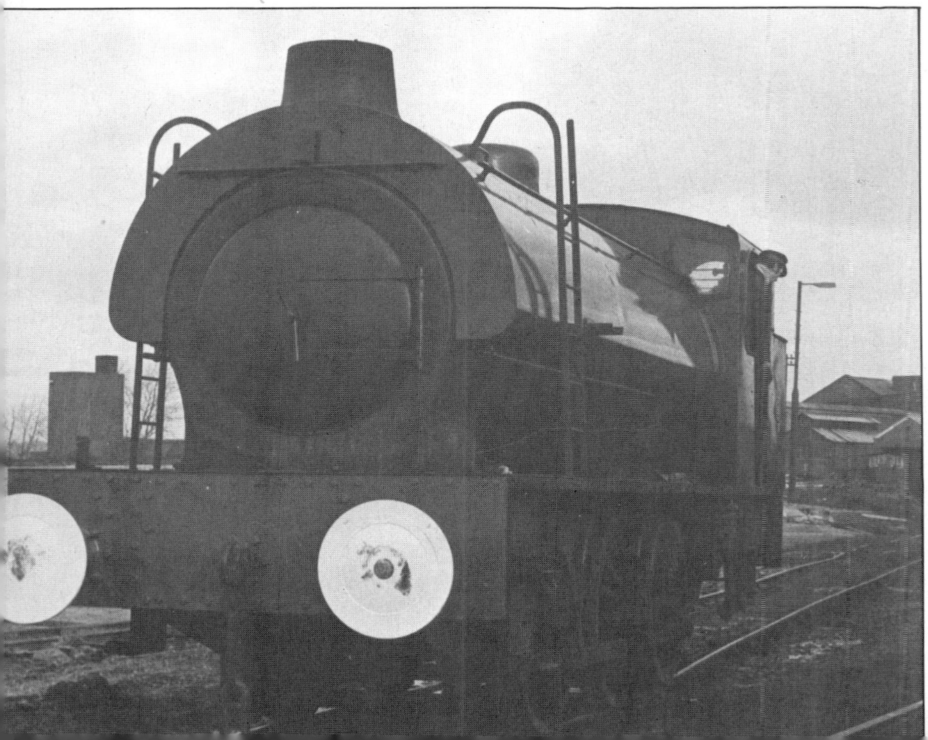

59. Beaumaris Castle, Anglesey.

60. This turnpike milestone is just across the fields from my home and I must have photographed it a dozen times. Each time I make a mental note to come back and 'do' it properly, with a tripod and oblique flash. Another idea is to photograph every milestone in the series, many of which still stand.

61. Civil War Society reconstruction. There are two ways to picture these events. If your primary requirement is for illustrations of period battles then close-ups made with the help of a long lens, in this case the far end of an 80-200 zoom, are called for. If you are trying to show the event as a history-slanted day out, then the spectators must be included.

62. Colliery locomotive at Wheldale Pit, Castleford. A useful record of work and industry.

APPENDIX ONE

Filters for local history and archaeology

Filters for monochrome

Filter	Lightens	Darkens
red	red, orange, some browns	blue, green
green	green, blue	red, orange, some browns
yellow	yellow, brown, orange	blue, some greens
blue	blue, some greens	yellow, sepia
sepia	sepia, some browns	blue, some greens

Filters for colour

Filter	Effect
Ultraviolet	Filters out excess blue in distant scenes. Protects lens surface from damage.
Polarizing	Clarifies colours and darkens sky at certain angles.
Neutral Density	Enables very fast film to be used in strong light.

APPENDIX TWO

Reciprocity effects on films

Though the relationship between the shutter-open time and the lens aperture should remain constant over a wide range of exposures, in fact it does not. With most films no correction for this *failure of the law of recriprocity* is necessary for exposure between one second and one thousandth of a second. Exposures longer than one second do need increasing, and as colour balance changes too, some corrective filtration becomes necessary. The only reliable way to estimate exposure increase and filtration is to send to the manufacturers of the film for their **Professional Data Guide**, which all keen local history photographers should retain in any case.

In the absence of the proper data, it is sensible to adjust the aperture to give the exposure of one second or less. If the lighting is particulary poor, and the subject does not lend itself to flash, eg a church interior, increase exposure by a factor of two if the indicated exposure is between three seconds and five seconds, and by a factor of three if the indicated exposure is between five and eight seconds. Naturally, it is wiser to bracket exposures in this situation.

Bibliography

Books

Aston, M & Rowley, T, *Landscape Archaeology*, Newton Abbot 1974.

Buchanan, T, *Photographing Historic Buildings*, RCHM, ISBN 0 11 701123 1.

Conlon, V M, Camera Techniques in Archaeology, London 1973.

Cookson, M B, *Photography for Archaeologists*, London 1954.

Deuel, Leo, *Flights into Yesterday*, London 1969.

Hasselblad (GB) Ltd, *Aerial Photography*.

Kodak in assn with Time Life, *Photographing Friends and Family*, 1984.

Kodak Ltd, *Applied Infra-red Photography*, Rochester (NY) 1972.

Kodak Ltd, *Ultraviolet and Fluorescent Photography*, Rochester 1979.

Kodak Ltd, *Preservation of Photographs*, Rochester 1979.

Kodak Ltd, *Photography from Lightplanes and Helicopters*, Rochester

Matthews, S K, *Photography in Archaeology and Art*, London 1968.

Nassau, W E, *Practical Photography for the Field Archaeologist*, Waterloo (Ontario) 1976.

Riley, D N, *Early Landscape from the Air*, Sheffield 1980.

Steel, D & Taylor, L, *Family History in Focus*, Guildford 1984.

Williams, J C C, *Simple Photogrammetry*, London 1969.

Papers and Articles

Houlder, Eric, 'A Recent Use of Photography in Recording Post-mediaeval Graffiti', *The Photographic Journal*, Vol 121, No 5, May 1981.

Houlder, Eric, 'Preparing a site or feature for photography', *Popular Archaeology*, Dec 1981.

Houlder, Eric, 'Photography on site', *Popular Archaeology*, Jan 1982.

Houlder, Eric, 'Taking to the Air', *Popular Archaeology*, Sept 1982.

Houlder, Eric, 'Demolition and Redevelopment', *Popular Archaeology*, Jan 1983.

Houlder, Eric, 'Recording a small excavation by photoplanning without specialist equipment', *The Photographic Journal*, Vol 124, No 10, Oct 1984.

Houlder, Eric, 'Photography at the sharp end of rescue', *The Photographic Journal*, Vol 126, No 5, May 1986.

Quick, G, 'The Photography of Relief Subjects', *The Photographic Journal*, June 1975.

Glossary of photographic terms

AE; automatic exposure A mechanism whereby the camera's own exposure meter reads the light and sets the camera for the correct exposure. There are several varieties of AE currently available, but the most useful for local historians is *aperture priority*. Avoid *programmed* mode, which allows little control of sharpness.

AE Lock A mechanism in an automatic-exposure camera which enables the user to lock in an exposure read from a more appropriately lit part of the subject, and then move the camera and use this setting for the actual exposure.

Accessory shoe or hot shoe A bracket, usually on top of the camera, in which flashguns and other accessories can be mounted. The *hot* variety includes a flash contact.

Airbells Small, circular blemishes on negatives or prints caused by air bubbles preventing processing solutions sinking in.

Ambient light The natural light already prevalent at a location.

Audio-visual The combination of recorded commentary, music, effects, etc with projected slides. Often multiple projectors are used to obtain a dissolve effect between slides.

Auto-winder Electrical mechanism to advance film.

Beaded screen A projection screen made up of millions of tiny glass beads. It gives a bright image, but only over a narrow angle, and is therefore unsuitable for any but long, narrow halls.

Bellows Leather or plastic bellows intended to go between a camera body and lens to increase the magnification of the image. Those which maintain the links between lens and body are designated *auto*.

Bracketing Taking several exposures of the same subject at varying exposures to ensure a usable result.

Cable release A means of releasing the shutter from a short distance, thus obviating chances of camera shake. Must be used with a tripod.

Carousel A particularly robust and high quality projector manufactured by Kodak.

Cokin A range of resin filters forming a 'system'. Users of the Cokin system and similar ranges do not need to purchase separate filters for each of their lenses, simply a small adaptor.

Colour Correction or CC Filters Special filters used to match colour film exactly to the colour temperature of the light.

Cibachrome A method of printing from slides, giving results of high archival permanence and excellent colour saturation. Cibachromes also give excellent monochrome reproduction of colour slides.

Compact camera A modern term describing a particularly convenient type of fixed-lens 35mm camera, usually with many automated functions.

Copy-stand An accessory designed to allow a camera to make copies of documents etc.

Close-up lenses Inexpensive single-glass lenses which go in front of a camera lens. When used with care and well stopped-down, they produce excellent results.

Cropping The act of trimming a picture, either with a knife or on the enlarger baseboard.

Data-back An electronic back for a camera which imprints data onto the film during exposure.

Dedication Not the name of a game, but an accessory designed to electronically integrate itself with the camera's exposure system.

Depth of Field The space in front of and behind the actual point focussed on, which is also sharp. It varies with the aperture in use and the type of lens. Thus a wide angle lens has a greater depth of field than a long focus one. There is more depth of field at f16 than at f4.

Emulsion The sensitive coating on photographic film. It can be distinguished from the *film base* because it is usually less shiny.

Extension tubes Precision machined tubes which serve the same purpose as bellows, but are not continuously variable as are bellows.

Exposure The act of allowing light to reach the film or the printing paper. There is only one correct exposure for most subjects, though some films, like colour negative material, have more latitude than others.

Film base The transparent material which supports the *emulsion.*

Filters Transparent sheets of optical material designed to modify the light reaching the film. Most filters hold back some light, and the exposure has to be increased. This increase is called the *filter factor.*

Gepe A proprietry brand of glass slide mounts preferred by experts.

Guide number The common method of stating the power of a flashgun. Also a method of calculating exposure for non-auto flashguns. The guide number, or GN, is divided by the subject distance, and the resulting figure is the aperture to use in average conditions. Outdoors, open up by one full stop, and in small, white rooms, close down by a stop. Always remember that GNs can be in feet or metres and use the appropriate figures on the focussing scale.

Hand held meter A separate exposure meter which can be used in the hand. Particularly useful for checking a camera's meter and often more accurate because it has a larger cell.

Haze filter A lightly coloured filter designed primarily for colour negative film. When used with *reversal film* it often causes an unpleasant brownish cast.

Hot shoe See *accessory shoe*

Incident light meter A form of hand held meter which measures the light falling onto the subject, rather than that reflected off it. Extremely accurate exposures are possible with intelligent use.

Infra-red Invisible rays which can be utilised to reveal cropmarks on aerial pictures, hidden details of paintings, and timber framing beneath cement rendering. A proper film in either colour or mono is needed.

ISO rating A way of measuring film speed or sensitivity. Each doubling of the ISO number is a doubling of the film speed. Older cameras may be marked in ASA ratings, which are exactly the same.

Lamitol A proprietry laquer which effectively hides scratches on the base-side of tranparencies and negatives.

Macro An often abused term which in reality means the photography of items magnified more than life size. Today, it is often used to mean merely close-focussing. A true macro lens is extremely expensive, and never a zoom.

Macro-zoom A zoom lens with close-focussing capabilities, usually to a maximum magnification of 1-4.

Motor drive Like an auto-winder but much faster, up to ten frames a second.

Multigrade Paper An Ilford monochrome printing paper which enables the user to choose the degree of contrast required in the print.

Newton's rings Multi-coloured interference patterns on glass mounted slides. They are eliminated with special etched glass, sometimes called AN glass.

Nicad Slang term for nickel cadmium re-chargeable battery.

Panchromatic A monochrome film or paper which is equally sensitive to all colours. Panchromatic paper is particularly useful for printing from colour slides.

Parallax The difference between the viewfinder image and the lens's image. SLR cameras have no parallax.

Polarizer A filter which passes only light vibrating in one plane. It is ideal for eliminating reflections, darkening blue skies, and increasing the saturation of colours. It only works at certain angles to the light-source, and demands a heavy exposure increase. In some circumstances, it can penetrate through layers of grime on old stone carvings.

Prime lens Any lens which is not of variable focal length.

Quickpoint mounts High quality glass slide-mounts favoured by experts.

Ready mounts Thin plastic frames in which slides are returned from processing. They are not suitable for projection as they do not protect the slide or hold it flat.

Reversal film Ordinary slide film. Confusingly, many photographers refer to reversal film as 'colour film', because until recently this type of colour material was the only kind used by professionals. It is still favoured by discerning photographers as it gives more accurate colours and is favoured by blockmakers.

Scale Any object used to provide a dimensional reference, but in this context a properly made one in metric or imperial measure.

Self-timer Delayed action shutter release.

Silica gel Chemical crystals which attract moisture. Very useful for placing (in sachets) with slides before projection to prevent the effects of damp and condensation. The sachet can be re-generated in a hot (120 degrees Centigrade) oven for ten minutes.

Slave Electronic switch which fires a flash in response to the light emitted by another flash.

SLR camera A camera in which the viewfinding is through the taking lens.

Synchronisation speed The fastest shutter speed at which a flash can be used. It is usually marked on the speed dial in a different colour, or with a symbol.

Teepol A proprietry detergent of sufficient purity for photographic use.

Telephoto lens Today, a term used for any long-focus lens. Originally, a particularly short long focus lens.

Thirty five millimetre format Cameras using perforated movie-type film 35mm wide.

Toning Treating a monochrome image, by bleaching out the silver image and replacing it with a chemical of greater stability. The most common toners are sepia, gold, and uranium.

Ultraviolet Invisible rays which cause excess blueness on distant views in colour. Also useful when deliberately applied to faint handwriting under controlled conditions.

Ultraviolet filter A clear filter designed to eliminate the effects of UV light on film. Many photographers use these filters to protect the front of the lens, as modern optics contain a UV absorbing element.

Zoom A type of lens in which the focal length can be continuously varied. Older ones tend to be of doubtful quality, but good modern ones are excellent.